To Roslyn:

Thank ya for all you help.

6-5-2017

TEMPORARY CHILD:

A FOSTER CARE SURVIVOR'S STORY

Edward, thank you for caring.

Edward J. Benzola
with Neva Beach

Real People Publishing
Fremont, California

Edward J. Benzola
5778 Bellflower Drive
800-Newark, Ca 94560
510ebenzola@sbcglobal.net
510-791-2452

\rea
rea

Cataloging in Publications Data

Benzola, Edward J.
   Temporary child : a foster care survivor's story /
by Edward J. Benzola with Neva Beach.
      p. cm.
   Includes bibliographical references.
   1-883359-02-3 (casebound)
   1-883359-03-1 (paper)
   1. Benzola, Edward J. 2. Foster children—United
States—Biography. 3. Foster families—United States.
4. Foster home care—United States.
I. Beach, Neva. II. Title.

HV875.55.B45 1993   362.734'092
                             QBI93-758

Book production by Comp-Type. Inc., Fort Bragg, CA 95437
Manufactured in the U.S.A.
First Edition

Disclaimer

This is a true story. A pseudonym is used in this book for my foster sister "Judy" in order to protect her privacy. All others appear under their real names, with their permission.

Dedication

FOR HENRIETTA L. BUTLER

One of the greatest foster mothers this earth has ever seen. If it were not for her strength and purpose in life I might not be here today. Thanks, Mrs. B., wherever you are. Maybe someday we will meet again in the place that was made for you; Heaven.

Acknowledgements

To Donna, my loving wife, who has put up with me during these very trying times and been by my side when I have needed her most; Thank you, dear. I love you, and I will never forget all you have done for me.

To Aaron and Amy, my two wonderful children, who put up with me even more than their mother because I'm home with them all the time; I love you guys.

My deepest thanks to Susan Garcia, who got the ball rolling, and to my sister Linda Servello, who found me.

To all my "new" family: Jimmy Servello Sr. and Jimmy Jr.; Nancy Bednarczyk and Little Eddie; Ray Bednarczyk, Cathy, Brittany, and Ray Jr.; Aunt Florence; and Tami, George, Daniele, and Eddie; thanks for all the love, hope and understanding.

My thanks to Tom Harris for his time, help, and encouragement while the book was being written.

A very special thanks to my editor, and now friend, Neva Beach. Without her understanding, patience, desire to learn about a subject she knew little or nothing about, and her expertise in the craft of writing, this project may have never been completed.

TABLE OF CONTENTS

INTRODUCTION

"You Ought to Write a Book"

In March, 1991, I had what seemed to be a pretty good life; a wonderful wife and two great kids (one boy, one girl), nice house, decent income. The only tough part was a ruined left knee from a freak job accident years earlier, bad enough to keep me prematurely retired and off my feet a lot of the time. But even the bum knee had its good side. It gave me a chance to develop a talent for oil painting that I would never have found if I'd stayed active in business. I was getting to be a pretty good amateur artist—or so my friends said.

Then one Sunday morning the phone rang. The next twelve hours changed my life forever.

Today things still look the same on the outside—family, home, income, hobbies—but I'm not the same Eddie Benzola I was before that call. That Eddie, I found out, had been living with only part of himself for a long time. The rest had been closed off behind a big, thick, defensive wall.

Behind that wall was most of my childhood. I'd been raised as a foster child since I was seven days old. From as

1

far back as I had any feelings at all, I'd been scared and lonely and *wanting*. I wanted people I belonged to, people who loved me because I was theirs. If I just had people like that, I thought, a real family I was born into, I'd know how to love them too. The wall got built, I guess, because after a while I couldn't stand wanting something so badly and never getting it. When that phone call came and I finally got what I'd been wanting—family of my own—the wall cracked wide open.

I went a little crazy at first. Even after I calmed down I kept being amazed by what had happened. For the first time in my life, instead of being ashamed and hiding my background I found myself talking about it to anyone who would listen. Then I was amazed again, because people who heard my story didn't act bored or like they were listening just to be polite. They'd ask to hear more, and kept telling me to write about it. "Other people should hear this," they kept saying; "this is such an inspiring story." These weren't just my friends, these were doctors, lawyers, psychologists, church people—people whose professional opinions I respected.

Finally, after enough of them had said the same thing I realized that it really is important to tell people what it's like to be a foster child from the inside. At first I was afraid my story would be too out-of-date. Things like that didn't happen anymore, I thought. Surely they don't still put little babies and kids into homes with violently alcoholic parents. Surely they aren't still passing kids around from home to home without any warning. Surely they aren't still paying so little for foster care that a family has to take in more kids than it can handle, just to scrape by.

Then I started researching and reading. I found out that things aren't any better today than they were for me and my foster brothers and sisters four decades ago. In California, my home state, the situation has been so bad that in 1991 a special panel, the "Little Hoover Commission," was commissioned to do a study of foster care statewide. Its report, *Mending Our Broken Children*, came out in April, 1992. Here are just a few of the things found by the panel:

> ". . . *10 children sleeping on the floor of a garage while 10 more youngsters were living in one bedroom upstairs . . . When the home was finally closed (six months after the discovery of the problem), the County removed five children who were still in placement . . . one of the children was determined to have been physically abused, resulting in a skull fracture and two broken limbs.*
>
> ". . . *a woman was arrested for the beating death of her 23-month-old foster son. Allegedly, the trouble occurred because of problems with toilet-training the boy.*
>
> ". . . *at the age of 14, (a youth), was forced by his foster father at gunpoint to have sex with his foster mother. The foster mother punished bad behavior . . . by dipping the wrongdoer's fingertips in scalding water.*"

The report estimates that this kind of thing is happening to about ten percent of the 81,000 foster kids in California—so about 8,100 kids are being brutalized or killed by their foster parents. Right now, in just one state.

The situation is just as bad or worse in every state I researched. Nobody knows for sure just how many kids are in foster care nationwide: estimates range from 300,000 to 500,000. If the percentage of severe abuse is the same nationwide, try to imagine the amount of terror and pain that some 30,000—50,000 kids are going through *as you read this*. You can't, of course. Even I can't, and I've been there. Numbers like that are so big they stop being personal, like body-counts in a war. But it's important for people to remember that each one of those numbers is a real child— especially the politicians and agency workers who talk so much about "the importance of the family" but keep doing things that pull families apart and send more and more kids into foster care.

Nobody knows the importance of families better than foster children, who can't live with the families they belong to, but can never belong to the families they live with. That's why I decided, finally, to write this book. I was a part of those big numbers once. The things that happened to me are still going on.

Mine isn't the most horrifying tale of foster care that could be told by any means. Thousands have lived through—or died from—foster care much worse than my own, including some of my own foster brothers and sisters. I'll be telling some of their stories too, because I'm pretty sure that not all of them survived to be able to write for themselves. Maybe one or two of them will read this and get in touch to let me know how they're doing. I hope so. I've missed them very much.

Foster children don't have to be beaten until their bones break or have their hands shoved in boiling water to be hurt. The pain of utter loneliness, of being forever different, not as good as "normal" kids in some all-important way, the terror of losing what little security you have at any time— these things are horrors, too. Anybody who grew up in foster care knows how they cripple and hurt us every day of our lives, no matter how safe we might look on the outside.

But if all I had to tell about was fear and pain I wouldn't be writing this. I'm one of the lucky ones. Why did I survive to climb out of that pain and make a better life for myself? I don't know. Where did I get what it took to do that? Some of it must have been born in me. A lot came from my foster mother, and I want to tell about her, too. I also had some plain old good luck; the firemen across the back of the block who always applauded when I sang for them; Dirty Ernie moving in across the street; lots of babies around who always needed whatever love I knew how to give them. Later, over four decades later, there was the good luck of being united, at last, with my birth family and finding . . . well, that's getting ahead of things.

I can't write a neat and tidy happy ending to my foster care story. I haven't found any ending at all. For every mystery about my past that's been solved, two more have come up. But now I want to go back to the place where it all started.

CHAPTER ONE

March 3, 1991, 9:00 a.m.

My knee—what was left of it—was swollen again. When that happens I know I'm down for a while, so I was spending the morning in bed. Donna and the kids had just left for church. It wasn't the nicest morning in the world, damp and grey outside, the house empty. I turned on the TV and started flipping around the channels. A week earlier I'd stumbled on a show about some people, brothers and sisters, who had been separated as little kids and just met each other for the first time. When I saw it I thought, "How lucky those people are. What a nice thing to happen." Maybe I'd find another show like that.

I was still looking for something worth watching when the phone rang.

"Ed? Hi, this is Susan."

"Susan! Hello. How are you? How are you doing?"

Susan is my ex-wife. We were divorced in 1980 but we're still friends and try to keep in touch.

"Oh, I'm getting around. Um . . . Eddie, I've done a 'you'."

"What do you mean, done a 'me'?" I couldn't imagine what she was talking about.

"I had major surgery in January." That explained it. I'd had a lot of operations in my life, as she knew; some of them on the knee that was keeping me down that morning.

"What's the matter with you? You've never been sick!"

"I have cancer, a very rare cancer." She was talking in her normal voice, nothing special, but her words stabbed me in the heart.

"Oh God, you poor kid." I felt terrible for her. She'd always been the tough one—I was the one in and out of the hospital. We talked for a while; she told me she'd had a couple of operations, didn't know if she was going to make it or not, I said if anybody could beat it she could. We were both trying to be encouraging for each other, but it was hard. I knew that Susan would be thinking about how many people in my life I'd lost to cancer—my foster mother and father, their son . . . she'd know how deep this news was hitting.

All of a sudden her voice changed. In a straight, high tone she said, "Eddie, there's something I have to tell you. Remember that time I found your father, back in '77 or '78?"

I could remember all right, but I didn't want to. "Yeah, but don't tell me HE'S looking for me."

"No, no," she said. I could hear her take a breath and then she went ahead. "Eddie, the person who's looking for you is your sister."

"What?" I thought my heart stopped, I really did: it hurt, a sharp, twisting pain in my chest. "What?"

8

"You have a sister."

I couldn't speak, my mind was blanking out, there was nothing but whiteness inside my head. Susan kept saying, "Are you there?"

It took a while before I could make my voice work. "Oh, God no, what now?"

"Eddie, it's more than that. You have two sisters. And a brother."

I don't know what I said then. Maybe nothing.

"One of your sisters has been trying to find you for twelve years. Eddie, call her. Call her. Let me give you her name and number."

It felt like a war going on inside my head. I kept going blank, then shaking and sweating. I had two sisters, a brother? Why did they want to find me? What did they want from me? What would they do to me? Susan finally made me write down the name and number. After she hung up I sat there staring at the piece of paper for a long time, remembering how twelve years ago I'd held another piece of paper, one with my real father's phone number on it. What had happened with him had almost killed me. Now here was more family, family I hadn't even heard of before.

How could I risk it again? How could I stand not to?

CHAPTER TWO

Doesn't Everybody Live This Way?

Mom says the Welfare Lady is bringing us a new baby today. I'm watching the street from the big window in the living room, waiting for them. New babies are fun. I get to play with them and hug them, and I can teach them to walk if they're old enough. I can help take care of them, too—giving them bottles and stuff. Mom says I'm good at it for being just four.

The grey car is late. Usually the babies come in the morning.

There it is! Turning the corner at the top of the hill by the store! I run down the hall to the kitchen in back, yelling as I go. "Mom! The lady's here!"

She's on her knees, scrubbing the kitchen floor with a brush. The kitchen has a sharpish smell from the soap she uses on the floor, a big, rough-feeling yellowish bar. "All right, Eddie. I'm coming." She's too slow, washing her hands and drying them. I want her to hurry up. The baby named Barbara is trying to stand up by pulling herself up the rungs of a highchair. Mom gives her a pat. "Barbara, you stay here. I'll be right back."

At last she goes and opens the front door. The Welfare Lady is coming up the steps with a blanket-wrapped bundle. Her shoes have heels that make a clop-clopping sound on the stoop. She holds out the bundle to my mother. "Here he is, Mrs. Butler. Paulie. Five months. You're sure you can handle another one?"

"Sure. Barbara's starting to stand already. We need another little one, don't we Eddie?"

I'm standing on my toes trying to see the baby but the blanket covers its face. Mom and the Welfare Lady are talking. I hear the woman say, "I'll be getting on, then. I'll be coming for Barbara in a week or two, so she can get her shots."

When I hear her say that I feel scared, and my stomach gets a twisted feeling inside. But I don't want to think about it, so I think about the new baby instead. The woman goes away and Mom carries the baby to the kitchen. She lays him in the crib by the table to unwrap the blanket.

Barbara crawls over and grabs the leg of my pants to pull herself up. When I look down at her I get the sharp feeling in my stomach again. To make it go away, I pick her up and hold her over the crib so she can see inside. I can just barely handle the weight. "Hey, Barbara, you want to see the new baby?"

Paulie, the new baby, has spiky, straight black hair and a red face. It's all twisted up. "Hey, Baby, don't cry," I tell him. "My name is Eddie. This is Barbara, and this is Mom. We'll take care of you."

—•—

Until they're old enough to go out into the world and learn otherwise, kids naturally think that other families are like their own. When I was little I thought all families had new babies and kids coming and going all the time. But at least I knew it wasn't any stork that brought them, it was the Welfare Lady in the grey car.

I'd come to Henrietta Butler in the grey car too, when I was seven days old. She was fifty-five; by then she'd born and raised three children of her own and fostered so many others that she'd stopped counting. Our house had a crib in every room, so Mom—that's what I called her—could keep an eye on the babies no matter what else she was doing. I thought this was normal, too, when I was too young to know better.

But even though I thought our family was normal, from as far back as I can remember I always felt like something was wrong, something important was missing. I also knew, without anything ever being said, that it wasn't something to ask Mom about. What would I have asked, anyway? I didn't know the words "foster child." All I knew was that I had an empty feeling deep inside. Having all those babies and kids around was a blessing, because when a new one came, it made the feeling go away for a while.

My mother was a living saint, taking on all those children year after year. The welfare people knew it, too. They always sent her the ones that nobody could do anything with, the ones with real problems.

My mother loved each one of them. Each one was special to her; she really *knew* them. Sometimes she told me stories about children she hadn't seen for years. She talked about one of them often, one special baby girl who was very ill.

13

The agency had tried every foster home they could find to help her, even took her to the hospital. But nobody knew what was wrong and nobody had any luck with her. She was dying, just skin and bones. Finally the agency asked my mother if she would take the baby and try to help her get well.

In about six months the little girl was plump and happy. Nobody had a medical explanation for it. But I knew it was because my mother's love for kids radiated around her, and the little girl could feel it, that she was really loved.

The Welfare Lady was always coming, in that grey car with the medallion on the side that said "Westchester Welfare Agency." If she wasn't coming to bring us a new baby, she was coming to take one of us to the welfare building—for "shots" or a "doctor visit." Sometimes that was the truth. Sometimes it wasn't. Sometimes it meant that one of the kids was leaving our house for good.

The babies and other kids didn't know any better, they hadn't seen it happen so many times like I had. But I learned early how to tell the difference.

When a kid was leaving for good, if they were more than very little babies my mother would go out and get them a new outfit to wear and buy them a doll or a new toy. "You're going on a ride to see the doctor, Barbara. Here's a doll for you to play with on the way." It probably fooled them, but I knew the truth and it made me sick to watch.

"We want you to look nice for the doctor," she'd tell them when she got them dressed. When they were all ready and waiting for the grey car, she'd take their pictures—always in the living room, never when they were getting into the car. Maybe she figured they'd know something was wrong if she took pictures there. Other than that there was nothing special when they left. Nothing went with them, no clothes or

14

toys or anything that might tip them off. They'd just get dressed up, maybe have a new doll, and off they went. We'd never see them again.

You'd think I would have gotten smart and not let myself love them, if they were just going to disappear some day. But I never did. I learned to let them go, and shut up about them, but I never learned not to love them and save myself that hurt.

If I did, who would I love? Who would love me? My mother did. I knew that. I had the feeling of that inside, there wasn't any question, but it wasn't her way to show it very much with hugging and things, not after you weren't a baby, anyway. And she was busy with so many kids to take care of and the house. If I wanted somebody to hug and love, it had to be those babies.

There was only so much I could do with babies and little children, though, so I learned early how to entertain myself. I spent a lot of my time on my own, mostly in the back yard.

The front yard wasn't big enough to play in, just a little patch of scrubby grass and a couple of shrubs. The house itself was big—fourteen rooms—plenty of space for everybody, with big bay windows in front that looked out onto the street. It was a nice family neighborhood. The buildings were close to each other, but it was still quiet, not overgrown hustle-bustle like New York city. (Quiet except for the "El"—elevated railroad—that ran across our street overhead a block away. But we never counted that noise, it was just part of the background.)

Everything you'd need was right in the neighborhood, like a little town. Our house was on a hill: a half-block above was the grocery store and other shops, and on the side streets bordering our block were the fire station, the police station, and the library, with some apartments and other family houses. All the buildings were solidly made; the police and fire stations and library of brick, most of the houses of wood, like ours.

The back yard was a little bigger than the one in front. It had a battered old playset and a lilac tree that I loved to sit under. Lilies-of-the-Valley grew back there too. They just came up by themselves every year. I still love the smell of those things. That yard had good dirt, rich dark loam, but hardly anybody tried to garden.

From our back yard, over a low fence, you could see into the back yard of the firehouse across the block. When they weren't out on a call or busy working inside, the firemen would come out back to sit in the sun or work on the vegetable garden they had there.

——•——

It's after lunch one day. I'm a little older now, maybe five, five and a half. The babies are all asleep. I'm out back sitting on the swing. There's a hollowed-out place under it, full of soft dust that I like to kick up with my feet. It's nice outside. I'm looking over the wire fence at the back of our yard, to the back yard of the fire station, waiting to see if the firemen come out. After a while the Chief and three of the firemen come through the station's back door. They wave to me and I wave back. Then they go to the vegetable garden in their yard and start working in it.

I sit there for a while, then I feel like singing. I sing for the firemen a lot, but I pretend that I'm only singing to myself. Usually it's my favorite song:

He's got the whole world in his hands,

He's got you and me, brother, in his hands,
He's got the little bitty children in his hands,
He's got the whole world in his hands.

I sing it all the way through. When I get done, the firemen clap and cheer. I like it when they do, it gives me a
warm, happy feeling in my whole body, so I sing the song
again:

He's got the whole world in his hands . . .

This time they wave but they don't cheer. "Hey, Eddie,"
one of them calls.
"Hey," I call back.

——•——

It's easy to write about Mom. It's harder to bring myself to
write about her husband—my "father," I guess I have to call
him that since that's what he was for me as a boy. But Mom
was the mother of my heart, and I never ever accepted him
as my own.

Henrietta Butler's husband, John, was a steamfitter, a
drunk, and a tyrant.

To this day I get angry when I think about John Butler.
My stomach clenches up and I go through the whole thing
again, like I was still a helpless little kid.

If you ever saw my foster father, how well-dressed and
perfectly groomed he looked, you'd never guess what a
drunken monster he was. He went off to work every day in a
suit and hat, only changing to work clothes when he got to
the job. His nails were perfect, he got a haircut once a week,

and he never missed a day of work. He was intelligent and good at his work; he helped design the steam system for the Empire State Building, and he helped to design our house when his father built it.

To be honest, when he wasn't drunk he really wasn't that bad. But under the booze . . . he made our lives hell.

It was okay during the day. The house belonged to me and my mother and the babies then. We never talked about my father all day long. Then every day about the time he was due home from work, the house would start feeling different. Neither one of us said anything about it. Mom would feed the babies, and I'd help her, then I'd play with them in their room while she fixed dinner. All the time we could feel him getting closer. I'd come down, and we'd watch to see how our dog, Brownie, was going to act. He was part German Shepherd and part bulldog, a really tough dog. But he was always the first one to hear my father's steps outside, and if he heard them a certain way he'd be terrified. He'd run and hide under a chair. My father got violent when he was drunk, and Brownie knew he'd get kicked if he wasn't out of the way.

If Brownie ran to hide, it was going to be one of the really bad nights. My mother would start to cry.

Next to Brownie, I was his favorite target. The babies were too young to yell at, and the other kids didn't stay long so he didn't have time to work them up into a really satisfying level of misery.

Three or four days a week he'd go to the bars after work, then he'd get home around 6:30 or 7:00, except on Friday nights. Fridays he'd come home closer to 8:00, because it was payday and you got paid in cash in those days. He'd go to the bar and take the cash out, put it right up on the bar. He wanted someone to try to take it so he could beat the crap out of them.

The dining room was the Hell Room. That was where he took it out on me worst. He had rules for everything at meal times, for the way we had to sit, what we had to eat and how much, how we held our napkins. We had to hold our left arm just so, straight down, and the only time it was to be raised was to cut the meat; then the fork must be held exactly right. Everything had to be so proper—but meanwhile there he'd be across the table, drooling and raving, crazy drunk. He'd yell at me, throw things at me, no matter what I did. Meals were war.

Thank God for Mom. After a while she'd yell at him and take him on herself, so he'd leave us alone. She'd let him go just so far, then she put her foot down.

The other Hell Room was the living-room. The rooms in our house were arranged so you had to go through my father's bedroom to get to the living room, where the TV set was. After dinner on his drunk nights, he'd go sit on the edge of his bed and scream curses at my mother. He was just waiting, because he knew my mother would eventually go in there, crying her eyes out, and say something to him. Then he'd get *really* loud, because he knew he got to her. No matter how bad he got you had to try not to show it. That made him worse.

The other kids would want to watch TV, but they were scared to go through there alone, so I'd go with them. He'd shout at me, then, with his face red and twisted. It was shameful, humiliating, to have him yell and call you names and not be able to do anything about it, not even let it show. I'd think, "Why do I have to go through this? Why does he hurt Mom that way? Is it because of me?"

CHAPTER THREE

March 3, 1991, 10:00 a.m.

I was shaking violently by the time Susan and I quit talking. My heart was racing, I could feel it hammering inside my chest. I couldn't get up because of my knee, but I desperately needed to move, to run, and because I couldn't, my mind was running in place instead of my body.

It wasn't only the shock of discovering I had sisters and a brother, although that was enough, God knows. But the only other time I'd heard anything about my birth family, it had blown apart a dream that I'd built a large part of myself around—the dream of finding my real father someday.

I'd found him, all right, or rather Susan had.

One day in 1978 she'd come home from work and told me she had some news for me. She'd found my natural father.

21

My first reaction was excitement, but then, to my surprise, I discovered that I was also angry. I'd wanted to find my real father all my life; I wanted to find my real mother, too, but at least I'd had a good foster mother. My foster father was so terrible that I had to believe I had a better father somewhere. Now Susan was telling me she'd found him—and I didn't want to see him after all. I didn't have time to wonder about this because in the next minute, Susan admitted that my real father didn't want to see me. He had another family and didn't think it would be a good idea to meet me.

That was it, for me. I didn't ever want to see him after that. It was fine for him to have another family and protect them against me, it was wonderful that he had a nice life. But what about mine?

Susan didn't give up, though. Later she talked to him again and he agreed to meet me at a diner, but I refused. I wanted nothing to do with him. A diner! I was his first son, and all he could give me was a little time in a diner? I told Susan to tell him I couldn't care less if he dropped dead.

Now twelve years later some woman was looking for me, claiming she was my sister. Who was this woman? Why did she want to find me? Part of me was sick inside with dread. "What's going to happen now? What do they want?" I thought crazily. "Money? Did they think I had money?" Why else would these people want to find me? They didn't know me from Adam.

I don't know how much time went by with me lying there, my head racing around in a hundred directions and my heart pounding like it would come right out of my body. "God, I'm going to go through all that again. My father's dead, I know he is. That's what they called to tell me. Maybe they found out I collect art, and they want to get something out of me."

Another part of me knew that was crazy, knew that what was really scaring me were the hopeful thoughts that kept creeping in. "God, if she's been looking for me for twelve years . . . maybe she really does care. Maybe there is somebody that really cares." I'd spent a lifetime teaching myself not to need anybody or expect anything from other people. But something in me still hoped. And that was the most terrifying thing of all.

It was impossible to keep lying there alone with my heart and mind both out of control. I grabbed for my address book on the nightstand and started thumbing through it to see who I could call. If I couldn't run off some of this tension, maybe I could talk some of it off. Just then I heard the garage door rise.

Aaron ran into the bedroom first. He's thirteen. Amy, ten, was right behind him. "Hey, Pop, how are you doing?"

The words came out of my mouth by themselves. "I have two sisters and a brother." Just like that.

They looked at me. "My God, I don't know what to do," I said. I held up my hands, and I suppose I had a strange look on my face. The kids ran out, calling to my wife.

When Donna came in the same words blurted out. "I have two sisters and a brother and I don't know what to do."

"Eddie, Eddie, calm down."

"I'm sorry. There's so much going through my mind. Susan's got cancer, she's dying. I have a family, and they're looking for me."

"You've got to calm down!" She was getting really alarmed.

"I can't! I want to go outside and run, run around the block . . . I wish I could. The anxiety is killing me!"

Donna caught sight of the kids' faces. They were stand-

23

ing there staring at me. She tried to get them out of the room, while I just kept talking on, telling her about Susan's call.

Telling her about it helped a little. The sense of panic eased up, but I still felt like I was being torn in two. "I have to call her, call my sister. But I don't know what to do. I don't know what these people want. I know I have to do something."

"You have to call, Eddie. Nothing but good can come out of it," Donna said firmly.

"Yeah. I know."

She took the kids out of the room. I took a deep breath and reached for the phone.

CHAPTER FOUR

Sinners Go To Hell When They Die

A new baby named Judy came to live with us. She was about six months old, a chubby little thing with curly dark hair, very lively and rambunctious for being so young. I liked her right away; she had spirit.

For a long time I kept expecting Judy to go away someday like all the others. I knew better than to let myself get too attached. She'd only leave like the rest of them. But Judy was different, she stayed on and on. After a while, I let myself get really fond of her. Judy was different from the others in another way too because her birth mother kept in touch with her and came to visit her sometimes.

My father liked Judy, he really favored her. He didn't yell at her when she was eating, and he'd play with her sometimes. I didn't mind that so much. It meant that I didn't have to get myself in trouble for trying to protect her. What I really did mind was when she had a birthday party.

I never had a birthday party in my life. I'd get birthday presents when I got up in the morning, my mother would say "Happy Birthday" and that was that. So when Judy had a party for her first birthday I got mad, I really got mad. The party was in the back yard. Her mother came and brought a cake, everybody sang and she blew out the candles. I have a snapshot of that party, with me standing off to one side trying to smile, but not quite making it. I remember exactly how I was feeling, what I was thinking to myself; "Why is this happening, what's wrong with me that I never get a party?"

A couple of times my birthday fell on Thanksgiving, when the whole Butler family got together. You'd think since everybody was getting together to celebrate anyway that somebody would think of combining it with my birthday. But they never did.

The Butler children were grown up and had their own families. I've read about foster families that have birth children and foster children that were close and liked each other. Maybe if the Butler children were closer to my age it would have been different. Most of the time they ignored me, but sometimes they'd say things that made me feel like dirt—things about me not being really part of the family, like that. My mother didn't make an issue of it, maybe because she knew why they were resentful of me. I'd been with her longer than any of the other foster kids, and I was more like her own child than the others.

I didn't go to kindergarten, and since our house was always full of babies, I didn't go out into the world much until it was time to start first grade. Then everything changed.

Mom wanted me to go to Catholic school, even though there was a public school close to our house. She thought

I'd get a better education that way. It cost two dollars a month—that was a lot for her, but somehow Mom managed to pay for it. It would have been a whole lot better for me if she hadn't.

She prayed all the time, herself. Having all those babies to take care of didn't leave her time for church very often, but she had her statues set up and she'd take down her prayer book and pray at home by herself. I don't remember ever going to church myself until I started school. Then it seemed like there was nothing but the church.

The first time I found out that I was different was when I started going to that school.

The hallways and rooms at St. Francis of Rome school were so high you had to tip your head back to see the ceilings. The whole place was dark, very dark. The classrooms had desks bolted to the floor in rows, and each one had a special long pole for opening the old-fashioned high windows when it got hot.

My last name was different than my foster family's, of course, and when the other kids found this out, they made my life miserable. At recess the sisters would send us outside to the "playground." It was really just the street; the Catholic schools owned so much property in the Bronx that the city let them do anything they wanted. They just put up a sign outside, "Street Closed," and no cars would be allowed to drive through. Every day the other kids would chase me around the street yelling "Orphan" at me, and other names even worse. There wasn't much divorce then, so if your name was different from your family's, everybody figured you came from a bad background—and this was a Catholic school, where there was all this talk about sin.

I wasn't very big and I had spent most of my life at home so I didn't know what to do when they tormented me. My mother must have noticed something was wrong, because that's when she explained about my being a foster child.

I pretended to her that it didn't bother me, but inside I was very upset about being a foster child. It started to make sense that these people were always coming in the grey car to take kids away. Now I knew that I could be sent to another foster home or an orphanage at any time. That was one time when I was glad to be Catholic because at least you could pray. And I did. I really believed in God, was a God-fearing kid, and every night before I went to sleep I prayed "If I should die before I wake." That's a terrible thing for a kid to say before sleep! Because then you'd lay there wondering if you were going to die in your sleep. What's it going to feel like? I said prayers of my own, though, asking God not to let me be sent away from my foster mother.

In some ways it was a relief to find out that I had other parents, birth parents, somewhere. At least I knew that the feeling of something wrong, something missing, wasn't just my imagination. Something *was* missing; my natural parents. I'd already lost one family. That made me frightened about maybe losing another one. At the same time, I began to think and wonder about the birth mother and father who had given me up. I understood by then that not all families were like my foster parents. But what *were* they like?

After a while I learned to shut up at school and pretend to ignore the kids when they teased me. I just stayed by myself. That way they didn't pay as much attention to me, although they never did stop making fun of me entirely. That first year of school I got every childhood disease in the book, too; chicken pox, measles, german measles, mumps, flu. It seems like everything happened in that year. My father was getting on my case worse all the time at home. I was learning about hell and sin, and I started to believe there was no chance for a person like me to end up any place but hell when I died.

The first year at St. Francis of Rome I was out of school so much being sick that I couldn't learn anything. I flunked first grade and had to repeat it.

Nobody tried to find out what was going on with me, why I was so sick and miserable all the time; they didn't really care what you did or how you felt at school or church as long as you followed the rules. None of them, not the nuns, not the priests, nobody noticed, nobody gave a damn. Somebody should have noticed that something was wrong with my life.

The only good thing about being sick so much was getting to stay home from school. Judy was growing into a chubby little girl, more and more like a real sister all the time. She and Mom were almost my only comforts then. The other one was music. That was one good thing the school did for me, showed me that I really liked music. We couldn't afford an instrument but I did get to play some of them at school. At last I found something I was good at. I got teased about that, too, of course; "Eddie's a sissy, he likes music," that kind of thing. But I didn't care. Music satisfied something inside me, like it had when I was little and sang songs to the firemen from my back yard.

I was seven and still in first grade for the second year in a row when something happened to give me something new to worry about.

—•—

"Put on your good clothes this morning, Eddie," Mom told me when she woke me up. "The Welfare Lady is coming to take you to the agency today."

Most of the time I don't mind going to the agency for checkups or shots. I like the ride there through the country, and it's a relief to miss school for even one day. But right away I can tell this time is different. Mom's voice sounds funny, and she has a strange look in her face.

The grey car comes early, right after we finish eating breakfast. I'm all ready to go when it drives up. Mom sends me out without waiting for the lady to come in. I know Mom is standing in the doorway watching us drive off but I don't turn around to wave goodbye. I'm trying hard to pretend that this is just another ride to the doctor's office, even though I'm not sick and I know it isn't time to get more shots. But if I act like it's a regular trip, maybe it really will be. So I don't turn around, even though I'm not sure I'll ever be coming back or see her again.

It's only me in the car. The Welfare Lady never takes more than one of us with her at a time. I watch the countryside go by, like I always do and after a while I start to feel a little better.

When we get there she takes me to the big playroom where we always wait before seeing the doctor. It has a lot of toys so we call it the "Toy Room." It has a lot of pictures on the walls, too, and one big mirror. I play with the toys like I always do there, but after a while I start feeling strange. I have the kind of feeling you get when somebody is watching you. I start wondering if anybody could be looking at me through that mirror. How can that be? I'm not sure. But I feel eyes on me.

I know about people who come to look at children to see if they wanted to adopt them. Is that what's happening? Would the people looking at me want to take me away with them? I try to keep playing like I always do but I feel like they can see right through me like glass.

I wait and wait but nothing special happens. When the Welfare Lady comes to take me back home to the Bronx I feel a little better. Maybe I was wrong about being watched, or the people didn't like me after all. The next morning is Saturday so there's no school. Mom calls me from her room. "Eddie. Come on in here for a minute."

When I get to her room I know right away that something's wrong. She's sitting on the edge of her bed, for one thing, and she never sits down during the day. She's always moving around, doing things. I notice that there's no baby in the crib, either. She must have put him down for a nap in another room.

"Eddie, some people want to adopt you and take you home to be their son."

I don't say anything, but my stomach tightens into a knot in my middle. Mom starts talking faster. She's smiling, too, but she doesn't look very happy. "They have plenty of money, Eddie, and a nice home in the country. They could give you a good life."

I feel like crying and yelling at the same time. "I don't want other parents!" I tell her. "I want to stay with *you*, I want *you* to be my mother!"

The smile goes off her face and she just looks at me for a while. Then she gives a nod. "Okay, Eddie. If you're sure that's what you want, I'll see what I can do."

—•—

Mom didn't say anything more for a couple of days, and I didn't either, we just acted like the trip to the agency had never happened. Then after school, she called me into her room again. She told me that I didn't have to be adopted, that I could stay with her as long as I wanted to. I thanked her and said I would stay with her as long as she would let me.

Later I found out that she told the welfare people she'd never take another foster child if they forced me to go away. She had a lot of power with them because she was their best foster mother, so I became their first exception to the rule that forced foster children to be moved around to different families every few years.

But how long would that last? Mom had stopped one adoption, but what if she couldn't do it again? I could be sent to another foster home or an orphanage at any time. The next time the grey car came I ran to my room and hid under the bed.

For the first time, I started wondering about my birth family. If I had a real family nobody could take me away from them. But where were they? How could I find them?

The questions kept gnawing away at me. They built up inside until one day I couldn't keep them in . . .

◄—•—►

It's the first warm day after a long cold spell so the nuns are letting us play outside at recess for a change. There's still some slushy grey snow piled up in some places. I'm playing by myself in the corner, throwing pebbles into a hole in the slush.

"Hey! Eddie!" I hear some of the kids calling but I don't turn around. Sometimes they go away if you pretend you don't hear. Not this time. The voices are closer. "Hey, we're talkin' to you, Eddie. Eddie the bastard."

"Bastard, bastard," they're shouting out together, then I can hear their feet running away and I know the playground nun is coming.

I'm not sure what a bastard is, but I know it has something to do with your mother and father and it's bad. All the way home from school I think about it. When I get there I go to the dictionary and look it up. Bastard. An illegitimate child. The mother and father not married. Questions fill my head. All of a sudden I feel like I just have to know something about where I come from and who they are.

Mom is in her bedroom with one of the new babies, a really tiny one named Donald. The baby's in the crib next to the closet. I go stand in front of the closet door. I know that behind it on a shelf is the box full of the family papers, like my birth certificate that Mom had to take when she started me in school. I hold the knob of the closet door so hard my fingers hurt. All the secrets about my life that those boys were teasing me about are in that box.

"I want to know about my real mother," I blurt out.

Mom is bent over, patting Donny's head to make him sleep. She stands up straight and looks at me with a funny look on her face. Then she says, "Your mother died when you were born, Eddie."

"What about my father, then? Why did he give me to the welfare agency? Why didn't he keep me himself?"

Mom sighs. "He was a very young man at the time. He didn't know how to take care of a baby. He thought it would be better if you went with a family that could take good care of you, because he couldn't." Donnie starts to yell and cry. She picks him up and starts walking him back and forth. "The baby's got a stomach ache, Eddie. You go find Judy and see she's all right, now."

I can see there's more she isn't telling me. I keep my grip

on the closet door for a minute. But the baby is yelling louder, and I know she has to walk him to sleep. I let go of the doorknob and go in search of Judy.

—•—

I was devastated. I'd started building pictures of my birth mother and father in my imagination. Now I knew she was dead, and he'd given me away. But the box of papers in the closet had more bad news to give me.

At our house the kids had chores to do around the house as soon as they were old enough. My mother wasn't a fanatic about neatness, but with all the babies and little kids around it took a lot of work just to keep things going. Not long after I asked Mom about my parents, I was helping clean house and came across the box again. I took it down from the shelf and looked around to make sure nobody was nearby before I started going through it. My foster parents' birth certificates were there, not far from the top. I started to go past them, but then their birthdates caught my eye. I'd known that the Butlers were older than other kids' parents, but now I was old enough to do the arithmetic. When I saw that my foster father had been born in 1892 and my foster mother in 1894, I realized just how old they were—she was sixty-two and he was sixty-four. Now I had something else to worry about; what if they died, too? Then I'd really be left on my own. I knew if Mom died first, I'd be sent away in a flat minute. Should I have gone with the people who wanted me? No, I decided. The feeling that came over me at the thought of leaving Mom was too awful. I would just have to take my chances where I was.

I envied Judy. At least she knew her mother. Her mother

even cared enough to visit. After Judy had been with us for a couple of years, her mother was visiting almost every weekend. I didn't like it. Partly it was jealousy that Judy had a real mother that cared about her, brought presents, took her on trips. But it was also lonely when she was away. I'd gotten used to having her around to play with. Playing with the babies wasn't as interesting as it used to be.

One Sunday I asked Judy's mother if I could go along when she came to take Judy out with her, and she said I could. I don't know what I expected, but she drove us to some bar in another neighborhood; I remember that it was dark inside and smelled like beer and cigarette smoke. There were some tables in the back. She told us to go sit down at one of them and stay there, then she went to the bar and started drinking and talking to people. Judy and I had to just sit there for what felt like hours and hours. We could hear people at the bar talking the way they do when they're full of liquor. I hated every minute of it. I hated being around drunks. I sat there thinking about how Mom cried herself to sleep so many nights because of her drunken husband, and I knew that Judy's mother wasn't any different from him.

If the Butlers died, at least Judy would have her mother. But my mother was dead. My father didn't want me. And the Butlers could die any time, or get sick or hurt. The babies just disappeared, now that I was in school and didn't know when they went away in the grey car. I'd come home from school and they'd be gone. The Welfare could decide to move you around any time they felt like it, I knew that. Would it be my turn someday?

As long as I was little, I was helpless. Some things get easier over time, but being a foster child was getting harder. Worse things were coming in the next couple of years. But I was getting bigger, too—big enough to start making some good things happen for myself.

CHAPTER FIVE

March 13, 1991, 12:15 p.m.

I asked Donna and the kids to leave the bedroom and shut the door so I could be alone when I called this woman who said she was my sister. I had the phone in my hand already, but when the door closed I put it back down.

My mind had stopped racing around so crazily. The panicky urge to run was dying down. Where was there to run to? I hadn't looked for this thing, but there wasn't any getting away from it. I just stared at that phone and tried to think. "I'm not going to get hurt again. I'm just not. I refuse to."

What do you say to somebody you don't know? How did you talk to them? I had to think, to figure out how to handle this thing.

It took me so long to learn how to live with all the feelings I had from my childhood. I could cope with them now. I had a good, strong wall built around my pain, a facade that worked fine. But as I sat there I understood that I was terrified that my facade might not stand up to somebody that was my own blood. I didn't know what a real sister and brother were like, I'd never had that feeling. And it scared me. Brothers and sisters loved each other, didn't they? I didn't know anything about loving people that way; what if they expected me to love them and I couldn't do it? Or was loving your real family something that just happened naturally, by itself?

If this woman really was my sister what would she know about me? I wondered. The idea was terrifying. What's she going to tell me?

I forced myself to stop with the questions. At last I picked up the phone again and punched her number, thanking God for pushbuttons; I couldn't have handled a dial at that moment.

A beautiful woman's voice answered, calm and clear sounding; "Hi, you have reached the Savello's. I'm sorry, but we're unable to answer the phone right now . . ."

Instantly I got a mental picture of her just from the way she sounded; "She's beautiful, she's young, she's vibrant, but nice and even-keeled." Then; "Oh, that stupid little beep is going to go on and I have to say something! Do I want to hang up? No."

The beep came. "You're going to find this hard to believe, but I guess I'm your brother. My name is Eddie, and this is my number. Call me back."

And that was it, and I hung up.

CHAPTER SIX

Three Strikes Can't Put Me Out

My foster father got hurt at work and had to retire. Then the night-time hell took over all day long. It drove John Butler nuts not to be working. For a while he did stuff around the house, remodeling and repairing, but then that stopped and he would just sit around all day reading his paper. When he used up the paper he had nothing left to do but torment Mom while she tried to work in the house and take care of the babies. Sometimes he'd disappear down into the cellar. That was a blessing, even though we knew he drank down there, because at least he wasn't getting on Mom all the time. By afternoon the booze would be really working on him and he'd come back upstairs, looking for her to curse and scream at. If I was around he'd take after me instead. I was turning ten years old by then and the older I got the more that man hated me.

"Why don't you get out of this house!" he'd scream at me. "I want you out of here! I'd do anything to get rid of you."

It was the worst time of my life. I had three strikes against me before I even got started. I didn't have a real mother, didn't have a real father, and my foster father hated me and wanted to get rid of me.

Then one day I thought, "Hey, but there are three outs to each inning, and three strikes for every out. I'm the only player on this team, so I get all the strikes for every inning. There's nine innings in a game, so it's going to be a long time before I go down." I also figured out that when something good happens, when you do something really good and it goes great, that's a base hit—and a base hit wipes out the strikes and wins the inning.

I called it the Three Strike Rule. I don't know if it all came together in my head at once or if I worked it out a little at a time. But from then on my Three Strike Rule kept me from going all the way under when things were at their worst. Without it there were times when I probably would have killed myself.

Money was always tight around our place. Now a constant battle about money started. Before he retired, my foster father used to come home from the bar on payday and he'd hand his pay to Mom. She'd give him back some to spend for the week and keep the rest to run the house with. All of a sudden, once he retired, he refused to give her any money at all. He had a fine pension and Social Security. But he wouldn't give her a nickel. He started calling her a thief, and accused her of stealing everything he got.

Mom could barely keep the house going. She was sixty-five or so and getting too old to have so many foster babies, but instead of cutting back she had to take more, just to make enough to get by. There sure wasn't anything left to give me an allowance. So I became a businessman at the age of ten.

I started by going around to empty lots in the neighborhood and picking up empty soda bottles. Each one was good for a two-cent deposit refund, once they were cleaned. Pretty soon I was making more than most kids got from their allowance.

It was so easy I started thinking about how I could make more. There was a limit to how many bottles I could find laying around. But it didn't take me long to figure out a better way. I knew a lot of people didn't want to be bothered to clean their soda bottles and lug them to the store, so I started going around to the houses and apartments and volunteering to take people's bottles in for them. I'd bring the money back, I promised. Of course, I figured that most of them would just tell me to keep it, and almost everybody did. As far as they were concerned I was doing them a service. Pretty soon I was making $5 or more a week. A candy bar cost a nickel then, and a comic book was a dime—$5 a week was a fortune.

From then on it was easy. One thing just led to another. Jerry, the guy who ran the corner store, was impressed to see me coming in with my load of bottles, all cleaned, every day or two. Even though I was a small kid, he could see I was strong and I could handle a lot of weight for my size. Pretty soon he offered me my first regular job, as his bottle boy. He paid me $2 a week to go in every day after school to sort and wash all his empty bottles, clean them up, and get them ready for the truck to pick up. On the weekend I had to go in earlier because there'd be a lot more bottles then. I was still bringing bottles in from the neighborhood, too, so with that and my salary, I was the richest kid in the neighborhood.

41

The old man wouldn't give Mom any money, but I did. Every week I'd give her the two dollar bills Jerry gave me as salary, and I'd keep the change I got in tips.

One day I was looking around the house for something. In one of the closets upstairs, up on the shelf above the clothes rod, I noticed a coffee can stuck in with the other stuff. I was curious, so I took it down and opened it. It was full of dollar bills. Mom was a great coffee drinker, so it didn't take me long to figure out that the can was one of hers and these must be the dollar bills I'd been giving her every week from my pay.

I went downstairs, where she was feeding one of the babies in the kitchen. "Mom, what do you do with that two dollars I've been giving you?" She looked at me in a teasing way that she had. "What do you think I do with it?" Then she admitted that she was saving it for me so I'd have some saved up for when I needed it.

The thought of that can full of money stayed in my head. On Saturdays I started going up and taking a couple of dollars out of it. All the kids went to the movies Saturday afternoon. They only cost fifty cents, so that left me a dollar-fifty to spend at Bertha Hamm's store. Bertha sold every kind of candy, Hostess cupcakes, everything a kid would want to eat. I was careful not to shop at Jerry's store where I worked. I knew he'd want to know where I got the money; he knew I gave my salary to Mom. I bought cigarettes, too. I was smoking by then; sometimes I'd even take the tobacco out of the cigarettes and chew it. I was really old, for ten. I felt old and I acted old. I was being a grownup, I thought, but I was also doing pretty childish things. I needed to act old and act like a kid at the same time. Chewing tobacco and stuffing myself with candy both.

Some Saturdays I took Judy with me. She was this cute

little thing, six or so. I'd take her by the hand and lead her to Bertha's and buy her anything she wanted. After four or five months, stuffing ourselves with junk every week, we started getting sick, so I had to stop.

Mom never did catch on that I was taking the money. She was too busy to notice, or too old to remember how much should be in the can.

All the time I was stealing that money every week I told myself it wasn't really stealing, because it was my money anyway. I gave it to Mom and she was saving it up for me. Even though I made that excuse to myself I felt terrible, rotten inside. I had to tell the priest about it every week too, at confession.

"Why do you do it?" he'd ask me.

"Because it's really my own money," I'd explain. I knew it was wrong, but I'd never admit it to a priest. I just kept doing it because it made me feel better, at a time when just about everything else made me feel rotten.

Once I got my job at the store I went straight from school to work, so I got away from a lot of the torment at home. But I couldn't stay out forever. About six I'd come back and run right up to my room. I knew I should have been studying but I couldn't. I'd sit in my room and cry, because Mom was crying downstairs, while he screamed at her. She'd come up later on, and she'd say, "Let's go over your homework," but I hadn't done any. I didn't care. Nobody in the school cared either. She'd say, "OK, everything's normal now, let's forget it." Then we'd do the same thing the next day. Mornings it would be "He's not drunk now, let it go. Act like it never happened." And by afternoon it was all starting over again. I was miserable all the time I was in that house. Sometimes thinking of the Three Strike Rule was the only thing that got me through the day.

People were always coming to tell us, "Go get him, he's up at such-and-such street. He cracked his head and he's laying there in the street." We'd go get him, but what I really wanted to do was leave him. I was too little, so I'd ask God to do it for me. Every time we had to go get him off the street, with cracks in his skull and his lip bleeding, I'd wish like crazy that he'd be dead. We'd walk up to where he was and I would be saying to myself, "God, please let him be dead. Let him bleed to death."

I knew I wasn't supposed to think like that. You weren't supposed to pray that your father would die drunk on the sidewalk with a busted head. It was a terrible sin to think that way. So I thought I was going to hell. That worried me a lot. We heard about hell all the time at church and at school. I knew I was headed right there when I died, no question.

Friends could never come over to our house because there was no telling what he'd do. I'd warn them, beg them not to. One time a guy came by to get me—Charlie Red, we called him, because of his hair—and he was waiting out on the stoop for me to come out. My father told him, "Come on in, Red," to get him into the foyer. Then he picked Red up and threw him down the stairs. Just like that. Just because he was drunk and he felt like it. We thought we'd get sued, but we never did.

I liked working at the store. Jerry let me sit around there on Friday evenings and talk with the people who came in to shop. A lot of them were old, and I liked talking to older people. It was a nice place to just hang out, warm, with a good smell from the wood shavings on the floor, since Jerry was a butcher and butchers always spread shavings around to soak up blood. When my mother came in to shop I'd sit and talk with her too, while she had coffee and talked with

Jerry and whoever else was in that day.

One day we were sitting around there with one of the customers, Mrs. Schwartz, and her father. All of a sudden Mr. Schwartz made a noise in his throat and fell over dead. He had a heart attack, right there.

I was sorry he died, but just being around a dead person didn't bother me. I saw a lot of dead people in those years. Mom's sister Minnie died, then her brother, both in the year I was ten. It felt like there was a funeral going on every month.

Funerals were nothing new to me either. Mom's mother had died at our house when I was five, and we had her funeral there. At one of the funerals back then, Aunt Evie took me up to the body and gave me the dead person's hand to hold, so I'd know what dead felt like and wouldn't be afraid. She worked in a hospital then, and once she took me there to see an autopsy. So I knew that bodies weren't people anymore. You didn't have to be afraid of them.

Another Friday night while I was sitting around, Jerry asked me, "Eddie, how would you like to deliver a grocery order? Take this order across the street. You'll be surprised to see what kind of tip you get. You can take her order every Friday." Sure enough, the woman gave me 35 cents that day, and every week after. Just to carry a bag of groceries across the street! I knew I was on to something good.

It wasn't long before I had a good little bunch of regular deliveries. I always made sure to stop and talk to the customers for a few minutes, because I knew some of them didn't have many other people to talk to. One woman, I don't remember her name, she didn't even need groceries all the time but she'd call in on Fridays and order anyway, just so I'd come deliver. Her husband had died, killed himself when his mother died—he stood over his mother's grave and drank a bottle of ammonia. After that his wife didn't go out much, so I was about the only person she'd talk to all week. One Friday she didn't call in an order. I dropped by her apartment anyway just to say hello, but she didn't answer when I knocked. I went back the next day and still no answer. There was a bad smell, though, so I got the building super to come open the door. She was laying on the floor inside, dead, already starting to swell up. I knew enough about dead people by then; I was sad, but at least it didn't scare me.

I got even busier when the store gave me a better job as a regular delivery boy, not just a fill-in for a few customers. They gave me a big, heavy bike to use for the deliveries. I was fourteen, and I was in seventh heaven. I worked hard to be fast so I'd get good tips. Somebody would call in an order and I'd race it out then hurry back and take another one. Each delivery meant more money, so I hustled. Some of the other guys would open up people's stuff and eat something out of it on the way, but I never did that. I was tempted a couple of times, but I told myself "I'm not here to eat. I'm here to make money." I made $40—$45 a week. I was in the eighth grade when I walked into Nationwide Savings Bank up on the corner of 233rd St. and opened my first bank account. I was a proud kid that day.

School was still terrible. I wasn't good at anything. There was no way to study at home with all the screaming and crying, and I hated classes anyway.

Except for music. Music was the one thing I looked forward to, especially after a new family moved in across the block, with a kid my age named Ernie—Dirty Ernie, we called him. Ernie played guitar a little, and I started playing drums with him. Playing drums was a great way to get out frustrations, I soon found out. You really have to move, and you can beat all your energy out on those drums.

In the mornings and after work on weekends I still tried to help Mom around the house, and started giving her $20 a week when Jerry made me a regular delivery boy. By that time I was old enough not to steal it back.

One of the babies welfare sent around then was a beautiful little girl named Francine. She was about six months old, a quiet little baby, and really sweet. I was helping Mom get everybody up and dressed one morning. When I went to get Francine out of her crib I looked in at her and saw blood everywhere, soaked into the mattress, running out of her nose and mouth and ears. I grabbed her up in my arms and ran downstairs with her. Francine was quiet while I ran with her, she never even cried once, all the way to the hospital four blocks away. Mom yelled to one of the neighbors to take care of the other kids and came after us as fast as she could. She couldn't run at all by then because of her arthritis.

Francine didn't die, but it was close. After they took care of her in the emergency room they came out and talked to Mom and me. Francine was a hemophiliac, they said, with a rare type of blood. She'd hemorrhaged during the night and they had to give her a transfusion. Luckily, they had the right kind of blood. The welfare agency knew all about Francine's hemophilia, the hospital told us, but it was their policy not to tell foster parents about things like that. Mom was furious. If they'd told her she could have watched Francine, kept the baby in her own room, made sure the hospital had the right blood. As it was, only sheer luck kept Francine from dying.

About that time we also had a little boy named Peter, around five years old. Welfare called him a "bad kid." Peter was the youngest in a big family, ten or eleven kids, and his natural father kept changing his mind about keeping him.

He'd send Peter to the agency and they'd put him in a home, then the father would take him out. Pretty soon the father would send Peter back to the agency, and off he'd go into a different home. The agency told Mom she could give him up whenever she wanted, if he was too hard to handle. But Mom wasn't like that.

I watched Peter, I got really close to him. I could feel how it all looked to him. All his brothers and sisters got to stay with his real family, so I knew he must be thinking, "Well, what's the matter with me, that they don't want to keep me?" He was so hurt, that kid. He would run away, and he was just mean. Whatever Mom asked him to do he'd say "No." Or sometimes, "Go fuck yourself."

Peter started running away the first week he was with us and he kept it up as long as we had him. I knew every inch of the neighborhood, so I'd always go out to find him. Many times I'd find him in an empty lot near by, this overgrown lot with bushes he could crawl under. Later he started hiding at the police station, out in back of it in a corner. This kid was smart. There wasn't anything wrong with his brains, and he figured out that the last place people would look for him was the police station. I got wise to him, though. Also, after a while I think he wanted me to find him. Because really I think he was telling me two different things, that he was angry and running away because he didn't have something he needed, but also that he really wanted to be found. I think he was like somebody who tries to commit suicide but doesn't make a good job of it. I'm no psychiatrist but I think that's what Peter was doing.

Of all the kids we ever had, Peter got punished the most. I felt bad for Mom that she had to hit him because it hurt her to do it. But she had to do something to control him. That just ripped me apart inside. I knew he wasn't all that bad, he was just mean because he was hurt and angry. One day, after we finally put him in kindergarten, the teacher told him to do something he didn't want to do, so he pulled out his penis and peed all over the classroom wall. That was the end of kindergarten.

I was helping Mom make the kids' beds upstairs one day when I got a terrible feeling inside. I didn't know what it was, but I knew something was wrong. I told Mom I had to go downstairs right away, and I ran to the kitchen where I found Peter in flames. He had set himself on fire, it looked like his whole body was on fire. I grabbed one of the scatter rugs off the floor and rolled him into it to stop the fire. The smell was horrible, sickening, and I could see the burns, the awful burns all over his body. I picked him up and ran to the hospital with him, just like I had Francine.

He had some bad burns, but most of the flames had been his pajamas burning. Peter came back to us from the hospital. Now we knew we had to watch him all the time. Finally the day came when the agency told Mom she couldn't handle a kid with as many problems as Peter. She fought it but she had to admit he was too much for her. She'd have to give up on him.

I was getting bigger and taking care of myself, making my own money. But the idea that she might get too old to keep me was still in my head, no matter how hard I tried not to think about it.

CHAPTER SEVEN

March 3, 1991, 2:45 p.m.

By New York time it was almost five forty-five in the afternoon when I left my message. The pressure inside me eased a little. Part of this thing was over. Now at least I didn't have to decide whether or not to return her call.

Donna came to the bedroom door. "Eddie, we're going to have lunch. Do you want to eat with us or should I bring something in here?"

My stomach felt like a rock inside me. "No, God, I can't eat, you guys go ahead without me." She looked at me for a minute, then nodded her head.

"Okay. Call me if you want anything," she said, and left me to myself. Donna is a really smart woman.

I stared at the phone as if I could get it to ring by sheer will power. Then a horrible suspicion struck me. What if she was sitting right there when I called, listening to me but not picking up? I know she must be anxious, she knew Susan was going to call me about her today and give me the number. So she wouldn't go out, she'd be sitting there waiting, wouldn't she? In no time I was sure she'd really been home and just decided not to talk to me after all. When it came right down to it, she changed her mind about the whole thing.

I was sure of two opposite things at the same time. That she'd heard me calling but didn't want to talk to me—and that the phone was going to ring any minute, as soon as she got my message on her machine.

Then it did ring.

"Hello?" I said.

"Hi. This is Ann. Is Donna there?"

"Just a minute." I called out, "Donna! It's Ann, for you. Don't tie up the phone, get her off!" I knew that was ridiculous. We have Call Waiting. There was nothing to worry about, but I couldn't stand to have the phone tied up.

"Relax, Eddie," Donna said when she came back into the bedroom. "You'll go crazy if you keep on like this."

"I know, you're right. But I can't help it."

I was completely manic. My heart wouldn't stop pounding, the pressure inside me getting heavier and heavier. It scared me. I feel sorry for anybody that has to live like that all the time. I had to go to the bathroom. "Nobody move!" I hollered out to Donna and the kids. "Stay by the phone, and if it rings, answer it right away." I knew better, but I couldn't help it.

I tried to watch TV but it was just a blur and a noise. My mind whirled around and around, too fast for the thoughts to really take shape in my mind. Maybe the whole thing was a practical joke, I thought again. I knew people who'd pull a trick like that. No, it was no joke. I did have real family, this was my real sister. At last I was going to belong to people that were my own by right of birth. I'd find out what everybody else already knew, how people felt about each other when they were related that way. But maybe they wouldn't like me when they did find me. Or they were just out to get something . . .

Again, there didn't seem to be anything in the middle. It would all turn out great, really nice—it would be nothing but more hurt and disappointment, the worst yet.

A couple of times I called the phone number again, without letting Donna know. Just to see if someone would answer. I don't know why . . . I guess I just wanted to know something. But all I ever got was the machine.

CHAPTER EIGHT

Too Busy to Get Into Trouble

"Let's start a band," I said to Ernie one day.

"A band? You and me?"

"Yeah. Why not? We can get a couple of other guys, there's plenty that can play enough."

Ernie started looking interested. "Maybe Mark? He's a pretty good singer, and he plays some guitar."

So The Emanons—"no names" spelled backwards—was born, the summer between grade school and high school. I was fourteen, and that fall I was going to public school for the first time. I wasn't afraid of going to hell anymore, and I was determined to get away from the Catholic school and everything that went with it. Mom didn't like it, but I managed to "fail" the entrance test for Catholic high school, so there wasn't much she could do. I didn't want to hurt her, but I knew I had to get to public school.

The band was just one of those ideas that come to you out of the blue. We got two other guys to join us, and Ernie talked his father into letting us practice in their garage. I took a couple of hundred bucks I had saved and sent for my first real set of drums from Sears, Roebuck. Nothing ever smelled better than those drums when they were delivered, that good smell of new pigskin on the heads.

In a couple of months The Emanons were getting audiences. That sounds awfully quick, but there wasn't so much to it. Popular music then only had four or five chords. All I had to do was listen to records and pick up the beats that way. Of course, I was still doing my delivery job too, three to six Monday through Friday, and all day on Saturday; week nights the band rehearsed and on weekends we played. I made twenty dollars a week at the store, plus about thirty dollars a week in tips, and then more good money with the band. Besides, I was so busy I wasn't around the house much, and that suited me fine. The old man was getting drunker and meaner all the time. He downright hated me, and by then I knew there wasn't a thing I could do but stay out of his way.

The fun really started when I got to school. Unlike nuns, public school teachers weren't allowed to hit students, and I made the most of it. I skipped every class I could and told off teachers whenever I felt like it. Some of the teachers were calling *me* names right back, I made them so mad, but they couldn't do much more about it.

Everything was great—until I got my first high school report card. I failed every subject. It killed me to see how bad I was doing. I even failed Gym! Those kind of grades said I was dumb, and that made me so mad I started really digging into the schoolwork for the first time. The next semester I started getting As and Bs.

The band kept doing better and better, but it was still a surprise when we got an invitation to play in a big Battle of the Bands show sponsored by Wakefield's Music Store.

—•—

We all show up at Ernie's too early. The Battle won't start until eight o'clock and it's only six-thirty, but nobody can stand waiting around at home. We decided what to play a week ago, but we're so nervous we start talking about it all over again. "We got to do something special tonight, something great," we keep saying to each other. As if one of us is going to have some kind of miracle in his pocket.

The show is set up so the newest bands go first, working on through to the most experienced. We've been around a while so we're next to the last. Last of all is our big rival, a band that we know is really good, with a fantastic drummer.

Mark looks at me and says, "Eddie, you gotta let everything loose this time. We're gonna need you to knock 'em out."

"Yeah, yeah, I know," my voice coming out a lot surer than I feel. "Just make way for me. Don't worry."

We go up to 233rd St. to Wakefield's Music Store, downstairs to the huge basement. A bandstand is set up at the far end with rows and rows of chairs facing it. In back there's an open space between the entrance and the last row of chairs where the bands wait their turn to play. People start arriving before seven-thirty. By eight o'clock the place is packed.

We stand at the back by the entrance, watching and listening. One by one the other bands go on. Each time they stop, we sag with relief. None of them sounds as good as we know we can. "We got that one." "Yeah." But all the time we know our only real competition plays after we do, the one with the great drummer.

I really start sweating now. I don't even get to use my own drum set, we all have to use the same one. A drummer gets used to his own skins like a ballplayer gets used to his own bat. How am I supposed to knock them out using strange drums?

We're on the stage before I can think too much, the song zips by. It's time for my solo before I even realize we're out there. I just open myself up then. I don't think at all, I just let my body do what it wants to do with those drums. I end it up with a smashing round on the two tomtoms—and one of them flies off and rolls over the stage to the floor. I start laughing at that, and our band is rolling around laughing while the audience crowds around the stage, clapping and clapping and clapping.

—•—

I always liked being in front of audiences since I was just a little kid and sang for the fireman across the back yard. But that night when we won the Battle of the Bands was the first time I got the full jolt of what it can be like when you really get hold of an audience. I loved it.

The band was really rolling now. We were busy every weekend, and I was hardly ever home. Even so, I could see Mom getting older all the time. One of the ways I still tried to help her out was getting the kids ready in the mornings. Most days I also walked Judy to school down the street before I went on to my own school, but sometimes she'd walk with her friends instead. It was after one of those times that a secretary brought a note to my classroom first thing in the morning. The teacher called me up to the front and told me to go right home.

"Why? What's the matter?"

"Just go home, Eddie," she answered, so I took off running.

There was a note on the kitchen table; "Eddie, we're at the hospital, come down." I still didn't know what was wrong. Something told me it might be Judy, so I dashed upstairs to her room. My stomach clenched when I saw her bloody school clothes lying on her bed, the little blue skirt and white blouse she was wearing when she left that day.

I don't even know how I got to the hospital. Mom was waiting. She knew how scared I would be so the first thing she said was, "She's all right, Eddie, she's alive and the doctors say she'll be fine in a few days." Judy had been hit by a car on the way to school, Mom told me, and she had head injuries but they weren't too serious. I could feel a knot relax in my guts. At least for now I wouldn't have to say another goodbye.

Goodbyes were always on my mind somewhere, maybe far in the back if I was busy, but never gone. People could leave, or just drop dead in the middle of talking, like Mr. Schwartz, or like Mom's mother and sisters when they got old. Mom and the old man were seventy-five and seventy-seven. When they died, I'd be alone. And I might be a hotshot drummer and an A student in school, but the idea of being alone was just as terrifying as it was when I was six.

Judy did get well and come home. But not long after, the thing I'd been afraid of for so long really happened. Judy's mother came and took her away from us for good. I guess her mother figured Judy was getting big enough to help around the house.

Her mother was still a drunk, worse than ever. I was afraid for Judy. There were times she'd call us or just come over, crying hysterically because her mother had beaten her up for no reason, just because she was drinking and feeling mean.

This went on, worse and worse, until one night Judy showed up looking like a grown man had been beating on her; both eyes were black and her whole face was so swollen she could hardly talk. Mom was so mad that time she took Judy's mother to court to try and get Judy away from her. But the system was always on the side of the parents, never the kids. Nobody would testify to help Judy. She had an aunt, older than her mother, who knew all about the beatings but she refused to speak up. The neighbors heard Judy screaming all those times, but they didn't want to get mixed up in "family business."

With no other witnesses, that left it up to Judy. She was fifteen by the time we went to court, almost grown up, but she was terrified of her mother. No wonder, either; right in the hallway outside the courtroom with the social worker and everybody standing there, her mother told her, "Judy, you say anything and I'll kill you. I swear I will."

When the time came for her to testify, Judy cracked. She wouldn't talk. The judge sent her back to her mother and told Mom she'd be arrested if she let Judy run away to our house again. That was the end of my having a "sister" at home. The whole thing reminded me, in case I was in danger of forgetting it, that the same thing could happen to me anytime.

I knew better than ever that I wasn't like the other kids, even though nobody called me names anymore. Because of that, I hated a lot of being a teenager. All through high school, any night I wasn't playing with the band I'd sit home in my room, while other guys were going out with girls, and cry my eyes out.

It wasn't that I couldn't get a date. Girls would come up to me and all, in school. I was a good talker, I had plenty of money, I was in the band, so that would lead them to me. But I didn't have any feelings about them. I just didn't get it. Most guys probably aren't sure what they have to do to get girls to like them, to want to be with them. Worse, for me, was not knowing *how* I was supposed to feel about them. I did go out with a couple of girls, one really beautiful girl, and did what I saw other guys doing, put my arm around her and so on. But when I had my arm around a girl it would just go to sleep. It meant nothing, I just felt a blank. I was glad the band played on most weekends, so it didn't look so bad that I wasn't dating like the other guys were.

At school I was taking things like bookkeeping, and business law, thinking I'd go to college after high school, maybe be an accountant. But my counselor kept telling me, "You're just not smart enough to go to college, Eddie. You should work with your hands. You're good at that." By then I had a B+ average, even counting that first horrible report card, but without help from the school I couldn't afford to go to college. I had some savings, but not enough to go without working, too. And there was no way I could do both at once and still live in that house.

I finished school ahead of schedule and graduated in January. The idea of going right into a job with no break was depressing, but it would be even worse to hang around the house and watch the old man scream at Mom all day. So my friend Larry and I got together. He was out of school too, and every morning we'd tell our families we were going into New York City to look for work. We'd take a train down in the morning, then we'd just goof off, go to X-rated movies, hang out. In the afternoon we'd go home and tell everybody how tough it was finding a job. We got away with this for two or three months, until our mothers figured it out.

We had to really look for work then. It wasn't hard, maybe because I had all that experience at Jerry's store. I got a job at the Longine Symphonette record company, filling orders, packing shipments, that kind of thing.

It didn't sound like a very exciting job at first, but it turned out that I really enjoyed it. Pretty soon they started giving me more responsibility, and that felt good, to be in charge of things and have people trusting me to do them right.

For the next couple of years life went on in a pretty good routine. I'd leave the house at five in the morning to catch the train to work and not get back until six. In the evening I'd play with the band or if that wasn't happening, go to night clubs with Ernie. The Emanons wound down, with the guys getting older and working, so when I got a bid to play drums for a good soul band, I took it. They were real professionals, playing all the good clubs and dances. I finally started going out with women. I still wasn't much good at showing affection in a casual way, the way I saw Ernie and other guys doing it. But whatever might be wrong with my approach, it didn't seem to bother the women. At work I was being moved more and more into the management side. It was clear that I was on my way to a good business career, so I quit playing drums and concentrated on getting ahead at Longine.

I should have known the peace couldn't last forever.

My foster father started asking me to get medicine for him when I was going out on the weekends to do errands for

Mom. He'd ask for bronchial mists and stuff for hemor-
rhoids. I didn't think much about it. It made sense that a
heavy smoker and drinker would have constipation and
trouble breathing.

Then I started having trouble with my own stomach. My
digestion was all shot and I couldn't eat. I got awful pains in
my gut. Before I knew it I was in the hospital for a spastic
colon. It got worse fast, and for a few days the doctor
thought they'd have to remove my intestine. Slowly, with
bed rest and eating right, I started getting better and they
let me go.

I hadn't been home long before the old man asked me to
come into his room one night and look at his rear because it
was hurting and burning him. He rolled over in the bed and
I saw that half the flesh of his buttocks had been eaten
away, his whole backside was nothing but deep, raw ulcer
craters. He was in the hospital in no time. There wasn't any
question about the diagnosis; he had colon cancer, and it
had spread to all his major organs. They removed his colon,
but even so, they told him he had only a few months to live.

It hit Mom hard. They'd been married for fifty-three years,
and I guess you just get used to each other after that long,
and don't really care how you're treated.

Even dying couldn't make the man human. By Christmas
they sent him home to wait for the end. He just stayed in
his bed, sometimes out of his head and talking crazy, from
the drugs they gave him for pain. He'd always been very
neat and well-groomed but now this all changed; he
wouldn't let himself be shaved or given a haircut. He looked
like an eighty year-old hippie, and he got meaner and
meaner every day. By then Mom had sent away all the foster
kids so she could tend to him, so they had nothing to do but
fight and scream at each other all day, every day.

I couldn't stand being around it. Most nights I'd go out to eat, then to some nightclub to hear music—anything to avoid going home. In one of the clubs one night I got dizzy and passed out for a few minutes. I didn't think anything of it. I'd been drinking, it was late, I figured I'd just gone too far. Then in early January, two or three weeks after the old man came home from the hospital, I was making up an order in the stock room at Longine's when all of a sudden I got dizzy again and collapsed. When I came to I was on the floor, people were bending over me and trying to decide what to do. A few days later it happened again; that time I didn't come to right away. There was an ambulance, oxygen, the works.

I started to get really scared about what was happening to me. At the same time, at home, the old man was starting to fall apart completely.

—•—

It's Memorial Day, a holiday, so I'm home from work. Ernie comes over from across the street. We're going out to the Jersey shore for the day.

"Let's go," he says. "You ready?"

"Yeah. But let's wait a little first. I want to hang around for a while."

Ernie shrugs and sits down beside me on the stoop. "Sure. What's happening?"

"I don't know. I just have a funny feeling, like something's not right." Anybody else I might feel like I have to make up some story, but Ernie's an old friend. I can just tell him the truth and he won't think it's strange. We're sitting around, talking, when I feel like I have to go into the house.

No particular reason, I just get this urge to check things out in there.

Mom's in the kitchen. I'm heading there when I pass the old man's door and hear this horrible rattling sound from his chest. I've heard that sound before, the death rattle, and I know his heart is stopping. His face is screwed up, his mouth open wide as it will go.

I run in and punch him in the chest as hard as I can. Meanwhile I'm yelling to Mom. "Call the ambulance. He's dying." I want to get him out of there. He's not going to die in front of her if I can help it. He starts breathing again and I can feel his heart beating. In a little bit he opens his eyes and sees me.

"Eddie," he says, in a scratchy voice. "My pocket watch, that gold one, that's yours. You take it."

That's so strange I don't know what to say. He must know he's going. But why give me his watch, when he hates me like poison? He keeps talking. "Downstairs, my big tool-chest. There's money for your mother to help her get on with her life when I'm gone. A thousand dollars. Dig down in there, get it for her."

I can't believe what I hear. He never gives her a dime, but he saved up a thousand bucks for her?

I ride with him in the ambulance. His face turns yellow while I watch, and he's dead before we've been at the hospital for ten minutes. It's only four blocks home from the hospital, but it's a long four blocks when I walk back to tell Mom he's gone.

Later, after the funeral, Mom and I looked in the tool-chest. Sure enough, there was the thousand, wads of bills, mostly tens and twenties, rolled up and stuffed under the tools.

I never said anything to Mom, but with the old man gone at last, a huge weight lifted off of my life. We had the house to ourselves, with nobody screaming curses at us if we wanted to go to the living room and watch TV. I would have moved out then if Mom wasn't so old. I remembered the promises we made when the family wanted to adopt me back when I was seven. She promised I could stay with her as long as I wanted to, and she stuck by it. I'd promised her I'd stay as long as she wanted me to, and I'd stick by that. I took over the upstairs of the house and made myself a little separate apartment up there. It was private, but I could still help Mom, and she didn't feel like she was alone with me right there.

One night when Ernie and I went into a restaurant I spotted a waitress across the room. She was gorgeous—a classy kind of gorgeous, not a movie-star type, just really pretty and with a good, warm look about her.

I nodded in her direction. "See that girl, Ernie? I'm going to get a date with her."

He looked at me like I was crazy. "No way," he said, shaking his head.

I knew what he meant. Normally I wouldn't have the nerve to come on to such a good-looking woman. This time, for some reason, I just felt confident. And I was right. By the time we were through eating I had a date to meet her after work that same night. From then on we were together every time we could find. She was Italian, with an accent I loved to listen to. She was just as excited by me as I was by her and we soon had a very steamy relationship going. She was wonderful. We never went out anywhere, just over to my place. She'd talk with Mom a while, then we'd go upstairs and make love until I had to take her home.

Mom was crazy about this girl, too. "I can die now, you have somebody," she'd say.

Even the ending was good. When her six-month visa ran out, and she had to go back to Italy, we were sad, but both of us knew it was for the best.

Mom was disappointed. I was starting to get worried about her. She'd been depressed ever since the old man died. All the energy seemed to be drained right out of her. "Why are you so sad?" I asked her one day. "After the way he treated you all those years?"

"He was my husband. I took him for better or worse," was all she said.

I didn't bother her about it anymore, but I thought to myself, "Well, I didn't take him. I never had a choice about it. Thank God the man's gone out of my life at last." But I kept it to myself.

CHAPTER NINE

March 3, 1991, 4:30 p.m.

I tried doing some of the self-hypnosis exercises the psychologist had taught me for pain-control. "Quiet your mind, Eddie," I told myself. "Let the sounds from the house and outside fill your awareness . . ." But all I could hear was the phone not ringing.

The afternoon trickled by. Amy and Aaron went out to play. Donna stayed in the house, but left me to myself in the bedroom. I was grateful for that. I needed her to be close, but not right in the room with me. I didn't want anybody, not even her, to see how I was feeling and acting. And if she was there with me I was afraid I might take this thing out on her—God knows I felt like yelling at somebody.

The world shrank until it was completely filled by the phone on the table beside the bed. Nothing existed but the phone, and me waiting for it to ring.

Waiting. That was something I'd been doing a lot of. It was hard to do. I'd always depended on taking action, being in control. But the accident with my knee had changed all that. I hadn't worked since I retired a year ago. I wasn't a manager of anybody but myself now. I couldn't even do things around the house, mow the lawn or build things in the back yard. I tried sometimes, but the knee always put me right back on the bed.

If what this woman wanted was my attention, she had picked the right time to get in touch.

What would have happened if I'd been like this when Susan first got in touch with my real father, twelve years ago? I was busy then, a success. I had my own business, I was moving to California to start an even bigger one. There was so much going on in my life that finding my father didn't fill my whole head the way this call was doing. If that call had come now, instead of back then, I realized I probably would have chased him down.

If she ever did call back, would this woman, my so-called sister, lead me back to him now, too?

I forced myself to look away from the phone, and picked up my left leg with my hands to swing it over the side of the bed. The pain came like a soft explosion, starting in the knee and blowing out from it. I didn't fight it, just let it happen like I'd learned to do. Picking up my cane, I limped out to the den and poured myself a beer.

Back on the bed, I gulped the beer and waited for it to take effect. Nothing happened. I should have known it wouldn't be that easy.

Donna came in with a tray. "Try to eat some dinner, Eddie."

"I'll try. It looks good." Usually on Sundays I'm the one who cooks, unless my knee was bad like today. She'd made

a meatloaf, with mashed potatoes and green beans; it was delicious, but I couldn't get more than a bite or two of it down.

"I'm sorry, honey," I said when she came to get the tray. "I just can't."

"Okay."

She came back in while the kids washed the dishes and propped herself up on the bed beside me to watch 60 Minutes. I tried to keep my eyes on the TV screen, but without my even realizing it, pretty soon I found myself staring at the phone again, instead.

"Ring, damn you!" I wanted to shout out loud, but I only shouted it inside my head. Donna was worried enough already.

At eight o'clock I told her, "If it gets to be ten, she's not going to call back."

This time she didn't try to reassure me.

CHAPTER TEN

Almost Dead is Still Alive

The drugs make it hard to tell the difference between being asleep and being awake. I'm floating somewhere in the middle, slipping down to sleep for a while, then drifting back up to half-awake.

I know it's afternoon because of the quiet. Each part of the hospital day has its sounds, and this is the quiet space between lunch and supper. Sometime later, clinking and shuffling noises make it through the fog in my head. I open my eyes. I recognize the fuzzy white and pink blur to my right as a nurse. Straining to focus, I see that she's holding a plastic bag. The drawer of my nightstand is open and she's putting my things in the bag; my watch, a book Mom brought, my pen.

She sees me watching her. "You'll be going to a different hospital now, Eddie."

By the time her words get through the fog in my head and I work up the energy to ask what she's talking about, she's gone, so I slide back into sleep.

They wake me up for dinner. I don't eat much, as usual, but they don't bother me about it. They used to try to get me to eat because I'm so thin, but after the first couple of months they gave up. After dinner two orderlies bring a wheelchair in. They sit me up in bed and before I know what's happening, they've got me in the chair.

"What is this?" I ask. My voice comes out strange because I don't use it very often. "Where are you taking me?"

"Don't worry. You'll be fine," one of them says. Already they've wheeled me out and down the hall. Everything is going by in a blur. My heart is pounding like it's going to jump out of my chest. I try again to find out what's going on, but they just take me down and put me in an ambulance and won't say anything.

When the ambulance stops and they wheel me out, the orderly says, "This is Bellevue Hospital. They're going to admit you here."

Now I really start to panic. I can't let them put me in Bellevue, everybody knows what this place is. I'm not crazy. But I know if I let myself get put in here, it won't take long for me to get that way.

—•—

When I'd started having seizures at work, after the old man came home from the hospital to finish dying, I didn't worry about them at first. I figured it was the wine I was drinking and the hours I was keeping. I'd been going out a lot, drinking a lot, working hard.

The spells kept happening. When they took me to the

hospital in an ambulance the doctors did every kind of test they could think of, but they couldn't tell what it was— some kind of epilepsy was all they could think, so they started giving me medicine for that. It didn't help, just made me sleepy and slow. I couldn't work very well and finally Longine's got tired of it all and let me go.

My weight kept falling and falling until I was so thin and weak I could hardly walk. Mom got scared and put me in the hospital. They did more tests, EEGS one after the other. Nothing added up to a clear diagnosis so they just kept upping my drug doses. Days and nights, then weeks and months, went by in a blur. Then the medical docs turned me over to the shrinks. Now came psychological tests. The shrinks kept asking me questions. But they never once asked me about anything that might really be the matter. They didn't want to hear about my feelings or my child-hood, any of the stuff that was eating away inside me.

"How often do you have sex?" they'd ask. "Do you like women?" When I tried to talk about things that really bothered me they brushed it aside.

—•—

As they push me down the long, dark hallway I'm fighting the fog, struggling to wake up, figure out something to do. They roll me into a big room full of beds with high iron bars on both sides and lift me into one of them. The bars make a loud clank when they slam the sides up around me.

"We'll take you upstairs to your room as soon as we finish admitting you," they tell me, and leave.

The room is dark except for light from a little window in the door. There's nobody in it but me. I lie there for a while, trying to get up some strength to move. If I can't get out of here I'm a goner. Somehow I pull myself up, over the bed-sides, and climb down. The floor rocks under my feet like the deck of a boat.

The hall is empty. At one end I see double swinging doors, the ones I came in through, with a clock overhead that says it's ten after three in the morning. My legs are rubbery, but I make myself run in the other direction. I see an Exit sign over a door, go through and down a couple of stairs, push my way out through heavy doors marked "Emergency Exit."

I'm outside on a street. My heart is pounding in my chest and my legs feel like noodles. I have to hang on to a parking meter for a minute. "You'd better think of something to do, Eddie," I tell myself. "Fast."

Out of habit I pat my pajama pockets. It's a miracle, there's some change there. Vaguely I remember Mom leaving me some in case I wanted to buy something at the hospital. Down the block I can see a phone booth. I push off with my hands to start myself moving again.

It's so late. Will she hear the ring and wake up? At last I hear her. "Hello?"

"Mom, they're trying to put me in Bellevue." I don't know whether she was part of planning to send me there or not so I have to ask her, "Can I come home?" If she says no, I'll just have to run and hide somewhere else.

"Sure, Eddie. You don't want to go there, you don't have to. Take a cab, I'll pay when you get here."

I don't stop to think how I must look, barefoot, scrawny, in my pajamas. The first couple of cabs pass me by. Finally I get one and convince him to take me to the Bronx. Mom's waiting on the stoop with her purse when I get there.

Mom took care of me at home after that. But going home didn't solve the question of what was wrong with me. I kept getting skinnier and skinnier. The docs kept increasing the drugs. They couldn't prove I was crazy, so they just said "This guy has the worst case of epilepsy we've ever seen."

One of Mom's sons and his family came to visit, the one with the daughter-in-law that hated me the most. She told me, "Why don't you go, get out of here We can take Mom and get rid of this house." An awful feeling of loneliness came over me, and got bigger and bigger, closer and closer. The old man was gone, Mom would be gone soon, now this one wanted me out. The pressure felt terrible.

But Mom told the woman, "I want to die in this house. I don't want to depend on anybody else. I won't be put in some room in the back of the house. I need my own home, and Eddie, you can stay here as long as you want, or you can go, whichever. I'm not leaving."

That was that, for the time. Maybe they kept pushing her to go, but I was sinking so fast I didn't know it, if they were. I looked like I'd been in a concentration camp. I was having two or three seizures, real convulsions, every day. Finally Mom had to move me down to the old man's bedroom. My weight was down to eighty pounds and I was too weak to walk, she couldn't keep climbing the stairs to take care of me.

"Mom, I'm dying," I said to her one night. "I'm going quick, and I don't know how much longer I can be here. I need help. Something's wrong."

She just looked at me for a minute, then without saying anything she went to the phone. Two of Ernie's brothers were doctors. She called one of them, Alfred, at his hospital. The next day he got me admitted there. They looked at the drugs I was on and said, "Who in God's name put this man on this stuff?" They told us we should sue St. Stephens Hospital. "They were close to killing you."

Slowly I got off the drugs. That withdrawal was horrible, the worst part of it yet. After two or three weeks I started to feel better but it took a long time to build up my weight and strength, get so I could walk again. The new doctors didn't know what caused the first couple of seizures I'd had— probably a nervous breakdown from all the stress, they said. But after that it was the drugs that kept it going and made the seizures worse.

In six months I was back to normal. The whole thing had taken about a year of my life.

I got a new job and started life over again. Mom was slowing down a lot; for the first time in her life she didn't have anybody to take care of. She picked back up once when the welfare agency asked her to take on two more babies. They had black twin boys that nobody was willing to take on. They knew Mom was seventy-eight, but they were desperate. I could tell she really wanted to do it so I promised to help out with them. They were cute little kids about six months old. Mom got a new lease on life for a while, but as soon as welfare found a better foster home, the babies left. Mom and I stood on the stoop and watched them go off in the grey car. We both knew she'd never take care of babies again.

Not long after that I found her sitting on the side of her bed when I went downstairs in the morning. She looked deathly ill, and said she'd been up all night throwing up.

"Take me to the hospital, Eddie," she pleaded.

It seems like I've spent so much of my life in hospitals. While I waited for her, I thought about the great time we'd had the night before. Judy was over for dinner. I had a date with Susan, a woman I was starting to get serious about. I knew I should leave for her place but Judy and Mom and I were having such a good time sitting around the table, telling stories and laughing, that I kept putting it off. This wasn't like me, because I was always a stickler for being punctual, but it just felt so good to see Mom so alive and happy again. It was one of the greatest times I ever had with her. She was still awake and happy when I got home from Susan's.

The doctors ran tests for a few days, and eventually said they'd have to operate. Mom was either very calm or very nervous the night before her surgery, making jokes, telling everybody to watch her stomach move like a bowl of jelly. The operation lasted hours. Finally the doctor came out and said she had three months to live, at the most; there were tumors on every organ in her body. "I suspected this all along," he said. "I just wanted to make sure."

I wanted to wring his neck. If he knew, why did he put an eighty year-old woman through hours of surgery?

We got her back home, but I could see that her time would be coming to an end soon. Meanwhile I learned I'd have to go back into the hospital myself—a different one this time—to fix a torn cartilage in my knee; the doctor said I should do it right away, while Mom was still in fairly good shape. That way I'd be back on my feet by the time she really started to go.

That was the theory. As it turned out, I was in for more than a week, with complications from infection. Before I even got out, they called to tell me that Mom only had a few days left. I made the doctor release me and hurried over to Mom's hospital.

Judy got there first. She said Mom had been asking to talk to me, but now she was in a coma. Her hand was clutching the bed-railing so hard it looked stuck to it, and I knew she'd been fighting to hang on until I got there. I wanted so much to say goodbye to her. I felt like I'd failed, not getting to her in time. But the nurse said Mom could hear if I just talked loudly.

"I love you, Mom. I'll never forget you." I must have said it a hundred times in the next two hours. I hope she really could hear. I think she did.

Henrietta Butler died on Saturday, November 15, 1975.

After the funeral the whole family came back to the house. When Susan and I walked in they were roaming around all over the place, looking at Mom's things and trying to see what they could take. When Susan went into the dining room she found one of the daughters-in-law taking out Mom's china. Susan told her that Mom had wanted me to have the china, but the woman just kept taking it out. "It should stay in the *real* family," she said.

Maybe there was a part of me that still hoped they'd accept me, but right then I finally admitted to myself that nothing had changed. I wasn't "real" family and I never would be.

The time I'd been dreading all my life was here. I was alone.

Me at seven when I started school at St. Francis of Rome and found out what a sinner I was.

I'm in the middle in back. That's Francine I'm holding onto, and Peter next to her in front. I loved all my foster brothers and sisters but these were two of my favorites, maybe because they had such a bad time.

Francine, on her way out to the Welfare Lady's grey car. She doesn't know it but she's never coming back from her "drive."

Some "real" children and some "temporary" ones on the Butler's back steps.

Merry Christmas? Mom on the couch in back. In front (left to right) are Judy, Francine, and Peter. Holidays can be tough in foster families.

A truce time at the dining table in the "Hell Room." Mom and John Butler, with Judy on his lap. She was his favorite foster child.

We had some happy times, too. Here's a bunch of neighborhood and family kids at the park; that's me on the right, in front.

Some of my new-found family (left to right): Linda, my sister who found me; brother Ray; sister Nancy; myself; cousin Eddie; cousin Tami; Aunt Florence.

CHAPTER ELEVEN

March 3, 1991, 8:00 p.m.

"Why?" I said. "Why would anybody do this? It's already eleven there, on a Sunday night. Why hasn't she called?"

Donna just looked at me. What else could she do?

I was getting mad. Was this woman going to make me wait until tomorrow, or the day after? Maybe forever?"

Around midnight, New York time, the phone rang and this time I knew. "Leave me alone, Donna," I said. "Close the door. I've got to do this alone." Then, "Hello. This is Eddie Benzola."

"Hi, Eddie. This is Linda, your sister."

CHAPTER TWELVE

Jackpot!

"Hi, Eddie. This is Linda, your sister." For a minute I couldn't see anything but black. I was wide awake but my mind blanked completely. "Tell me about yourself," she said right away.

That was all it took. I started talking and once I got started I couldn't stop. I just couldn't stop. I rattled on about Donna and the kids, our beautiful house, my early retirement, my art collection, my oil painting. I didn't talk about my childhood or any of the other hard things, I just talked about the positive side, making myself look as good as I could. I went on and on. I knew I was blurting out too much. It had me really upset because I wanted to stop talking so I could hear from her too, but my need to keep talking was too big.

She didn't try to say much, just let me go on as long as I

needed to. I think that's when I started to trust her. I really started to believe she was my sister. She didn't object or try to stop me, she was acting like I always thought a real sister would, accepting me for what I was. All day long I'd been terrified by the fear that I'd get the family I always wanted, only to find they didn't like me, wouldn't want me for a brother. But this woman Linda was letting me say whatever I wanted and as far as I could tell, she didn't think I was nuts for talking on and on. That's what real family does, they take each other as they are. I don't have the words to describe how good that felt, to trust her.

When I finally ran down enough for her to get a word in, she said, "How could I have a brother for all these years and I never met him?" I heard real hurt in her voice.

"How did you find me?" I asked.

"It took a long time," she told me. "For years I was looking for Benzolas. But I never could find any."

"I know. I used to travel in my business and for years whenever I got to a new city I'd look in the phone book for Benzolas. I never found any either. The reason why is because my real father's last name wasn't Benzola, it was Bednarczyk. I finally got to see my real birth certificate and that name was on it. Before that they always showed me a fake birth certificate. My natural mother's name was Lillian Barry, my father was Edward John Bednarczyk, and I was Edward John Benzola. There I was going through life thinking I was Italian when I was really Polish. I think they probably gave me a different name so I wouldn't be able to find my natural parents."

"When Susan found Dad in '78, she gave him the address in Mamaroneck, where you two lived," Linda said. "I'd drive there and park outside the building, wondering if I'd see you. It was silly, I suppose. I didn't even know what you looked like. But I didn't have the nerve to go knock on the door."

"Maybe you did see me, for that one year. But Susan and I moved to California in '79."

"So I found out. But not until yesterday. See, I'd search for you for a while," she said, "then I'd give up until something would make me start looking again. Then yesterday I decided I'd knock on doors along that block and see if anybody knew about a Benzola family. Nobody did. Finally I got up my nerve and went to your address itself. The landlord said sure, he knew you and Susan but you were gone. Then he told me that Susan's parents, the Garcias, still lived nearby and gave me their address. I drove right over there and that's how I finally found you, through them. So I called you."

Linda and I must have talked for two or three hours at least. She told me about Maud, who was my father's wife and her mother. Of course, since Linda and I had different mothers, we were only half-sister and brother, but to me she didn't feel like half of anything. She told me about her (our) sister and brother, Nancy and Ray, and all my nieces, nephews, cousins, and an aunt. But the most amazing part was finding all the parallels between my father and me, and how near I'd sometimes been to him and all these relatives without ever knowing it.

My natural father and I both had medical problems that almost killed us in 1983. Both of us retired early for health reasons. Both of us took up oil painting as a hobby. We both fell in love with women when they were fifteen and had to wait until they were old enough to marry them. He worked at the Chevrolet plant in Tarrytown; I used to be fascinated with that plant and would go hang out and watch the workers. He and his family lived not far from the Butler's where I grew up; his kids and I were probably at some of the same big dances in the neighborhood as teenagers—I might even have teased my sisters or, and this thought really made me wince, maybe I even asked one of them for a date.

These things came out one at a time, as Linda and I talked and talked into the night. "The Butler's had a grown son we used to visit in Brewster Heights," I happened to mention. "We'd go there to visit fairly often."

"Where in Brewster Heights?" Linda demanded. "What address?"

When I told her she gasped. "That's around the block from my aunt's! Dad used to take us over there all the time. We *know* that Butler family. Not your foster parents, but that son and his family."

"Well, that's my foster mother's youngest child."

"I can't believe this."

That's how we both felt, that it was incredible how our paths had crossed without our knowing it. It was so strange to find out how close to each other we'd been, how we might have met already. But it hurt. It also made me madder than ever at the stupid system that hid my records so I couldn't find out about my family and they couldn't find me. It was *my* life, not the welfare agency's, *my* history. What gave them the right to keep secrets? They talk about "protecting" the people involved, meaning the birth parents of foster kids and their families. But what about the kids themselves, like me? I could have found my birth family fifteen years earlier.

Linda and I knew we couldn't just talk all night, but before we hung up I knew I had to bring up the one subject we'd been avoiding. I was pretty sure my father was dead, but I had to be certain. "Linda, I have to ask you. Is my father alive?"

"No, he's dead."

"Tell me. How did he die?"

"Eddie, I don't think we should talk about it until you come here. I don't want to on the phone because it hurts me to talk about it still."

"You can be sure I'll come. It might take a couple of weeks to get everything organized here, but I'll be there as soon as I can."

When I hung up I felt so much peace in my heart. For the first time I felt I knew what love is. Something that had been missing in me wasn't missing anymore, and I knew that now I could be much better with my wife and kids.

Donna wanted to go to bed then, she had to get up and go to work the next morning, but I needed to relive the call for a while. We sat there talking for about twenty minutes, then the phone rang again.

"Hi, I'm your sister Nancy," a woman said. Her voice was very harsh, tough sounding. "Linda called and told me she found you. How strong are you?"

Her tone of voice raised my hackles. Well, I thought, two can play the tough-guy game. "I'm extremely strong," I assured her flatly.

"Do you think you can take the truth?"

"Honey, there isn't anything I can't take."

"I have to tell you the truth. I know Linda's told you all these wonderful things about your father, what a wonderful man he was . . . I want to tell you the real story. You think you can take it?" she asked again. The anger in her voice was unbelievably strong. I told her to go ahead.

"I want to tell you our father was a very mean person. He liked to drink. I was his baby, he liked me the best. Do you know how he died?"

"No. I know he's dead."

"He killed himself. He took a shotgun and just blew himself away. He did it because you refused to see him, when your wife Susan found him."

I was furious. "Just hold it right there. I don't need this crap. He didn't kill himself over me. He's the one who refused to see me until Susan argued him into it. Then he would only agree to meet me in a diner. That's why I wouldn't have anything to do with him. He waited five years after that to kill himself—if he wanted to see me he could have found me any time and cleared his conscience. So don't try laying the blame on me. I won't take it." It was obvious by then that the woman was drunk; Linda had mentioned Nancy had emotional problems. She'd been the one who found my father's body, and she'd been his pet, just like she said, so it tore her up pretty badly.

"Listen, Nancy," I said. " It's been a long night. I can't talk any longer. I've got to hang up."

Obviously my new-found family had its own complications. But even Nancy's attempt to hurt me couldn't ruin my happiness. My connection with Linda had been too good, too strong, and I could hardly wait to go back east and see her.

CHAPTER THIRTEEN

Face to Face

As the plane got closer and closer to New York I couldn't sit still. I kept having to get up and walk to the back of the plane just to wear off some of my nervousness. On one of the trips back a friendly looking stewardess said something about how hard it could be to sit through such a long trip. I told her where I was going and why. She looked at me with a serious expression for a minute, and I could tell she was touched by my story. Then she smiled. "It will be fine, you'll see," she assured me.

Donna had been amazingly patient through everything, right from the beginning. It couldn't have been easy. It had been a crazy three weeks since Linda's first call. We talked almost every day—my phone bill was through the roof. All my energy, all my thoughts and feelings were focused on my new family across the continent. When I stopped long enough to think about anything else, I'd realized how tough that must be for Donna. But she never failed to come through.

At the same time I was talking to Linda on the phone every day, I was telling my story to anybody who'd stand still long enough. I mean *anybody*—I'd turn to the person behind me in the supermarket checkout line and start talking. "You know what happened to me? I never had a family of my own in my life, until last week when my real sister tracked me down . . ." I couldn't stop, and I didn't care who I was blabbing to. Sometimes Donna would get embarrassed. "Stop doing that!" she'd say. "I can't," I'd tell her.

Now on the plane something awful occurred to me. "But how will I know who they are?" I asked in a new panic. "We've never met. What if we don't find each other."

"You'll know, Eddie. Don't worry. It will be fine," she said, for the thousandth time.

And it was. I knew Linda the minute I saw her at the airport. Neither one of us made a big fuss, but I knew that inside she was just as excited as I was to finally be together. And we'd been talking on the phone so much we immediately felt comfortable with each other.

I've talked a lot about wanting a family. Mostly I've talked about my birth parents and later about my sister Linda, then Nancy. In New York I realized how big the word "family" is, for most people. It doesn't just mean parents and siblings, but all the other relatives—aunts, uncles, cousins, grandparents, even old family friends. That week I met them all. Our visit included Easter weekend; my new aunt Florence threw one of her famous family feasts. All day, a steady crowd streamed in and out of her house, every one of them eager to see the long-lost Eddie and his wife.

Each new person filled a little bit more of the empty space

inside me. It was fantastic, but it was hard. When you've had your family since you were born you have a lifetime to get to know who everybody is. I had a week. A hundred times I thanked God we'd brought along a video camera. It was almost never out of Donna's hands. Donna was a tiger through all of it, not just my camera operator but chief investigator. Time after time she'd sense that somebody was holding back something they knew about me and she'd go after it.

One of the toughest things was seeing pictures of my real father and mother for the first time.

Early on, at Aunt Florence's house, she brought out a snapshot of my father and his two brothers. Without her telling me, I immediately knew which one of the three men in the picture was him. He was about twenty years old when it was taken, and he looked very much like I did at that age.

Whenever we visited a new part of the family they'd show me pictures of him. Every time, it hurt me to see his face. Being so close to his life there, and seeing him in photographs made him real. I felt sadder than ever that I'd never gotten to meet him in person. Everybody talked about him, shared their memories about growing up with him. I wanted to hear it, but it hurt.

My father's wife Maud was the one who showed me the picture of my mother. Maud was born and raised in England, and has a low, sweet voice with an English accent. When she saw me she immediately got tears in her eyes because I looked so much like my father at that age. Donna started asking questions about my birth mother. Finally Maud went into another room. After a while she came back and handed me a picture. "This is Lillian Barry, Eddie."

I stared hard at it. It was just an ordinary family kind of snapshot of a pretty young woman sitting in a limousine on her way to a wedding, just the top part of her. She was smiling. Her cheeks looked rosy and she had some sort of little hat on, probably for the wedding.

I tried my best, but I couldn't make her feel real. It was easier with my father, I knew a lot about him, was meeting his family. But I couldn't feel like I knew her at all. I'd always wanted a mother. All of a sudden here I had one, except I didn't. I had nothing but this little picture, and it wasn't enough, it was worse than nothing in a way.

"Did you know her?" Donna asked Maud.

"Yes," Maud admitted. She obviously didn't want to talk about it, but Donna kept pushing. "We weren't friends," Maud finally said. "She used to hang out in a bar in Yonkers where your father went, always trying to see him. Even after he and I were married she kept coming around for a long time."

I had so many questions. Why did they give me up? What happened to my mother? Did my father really think I'd died when I was born? Why did he keep her picture all his life?

Slowly a few pieces of information came together. But never all of them. People kept saying "Leave it alone. You've been hurt enough already, why let yourself get hurt anymore?"

Of course that could only mean there was something hurtful about the truth. And even though nobody would come right out, the bits and pieces and hints started coming together. Donna and I put together some answers we're fairly sure are true: My father did know I was alive. My mother knew where I was, with the Butlers. I was never released for adoption until I was seven because my mother kept hoping she'd get back together with my father. She only gave me up for good when he married Maud, instead. She might have been married to somebody else when I was born, to a man named Benzola. None of this was certain, but it seemed likely.

But we could never get an answer to the biggest question; was my mother still alive? "Probably not, she was never very well and it's been a long time," was the closest anybody came.

—•—

The only one I didn't meet in those first few days was my other sister Nancy. All through the weeks, talking to Linda on the phone, I didn't tell her about Nancy's call, or about her saying my father had committed suicide.

The first night in New York, as soon as Linda and I got to her house, I had confronted her with it. "My father killed himself, didn't he? Why in God's name didn't you tell me so?"

"Who told you? How did you find out?"

I told her about Nancy's phone call. She was furious. Later she called Maud, then Nancy, and accused Nancy of just wanting to be the first one to tell me. They all went around and around behind the scenes, wrangling with each other—it was my first taste of what families can get into with each other. I'd had this idea about families in my head all my life, how wonderful people were to each other when they were really related to each other. Now I was starting to find out about the stupid, moronic stuff that really goes on in families sometimes.

Our time kept getting shorter. Nancy still wasn't too anxious to meet me. I guess they convinced her she should at least be introduced, though, because the night before Donna and I left, there was a fantastic party. One big final get-together. The whole family—even Nancy—came to my brother Ray's house.

We went off and talked together. She was sorry she hurt me, but I told her it was all right. I knew my father was no hero, I assured her. Even though what she said gave me a lot of pain, I truly appreciated knowing the truth, and thanked her for that. Both of us felt better after talking. I hoped that at least one hole in the family's relationships was healed.

Everybody brought pictures to the party to show me, and through the evening they brought out their memories, too, and shared those. Ray went to the garage and after a while he came back with something my father had invented—a gadget for fishermen that lets them know when they've got a strike. In a kind of ceremony, he gave each of us one. It was the first time anybody'd seen the "strike alert" since our father killed himself. That brought out some more memories, of how he refused to sell the invention to a manufacturer who could do something with it. My family smiled and shook their heads as they remembered how stubborn he was. He'd go fishing and sell dozens of the things, but always just enough to afford to keep making a few more.

When it was time to leave I asked everybody to please wait a minute. My heart was so full I wanted to say something, so I made a sort of speech. "I'm so proud of having you all for a family. Our father did a good job. He wasn't perfect, but nobody is perfect, and I can see how much he gave each one of you. I understand why he did what he did and gave me up, and I forgive him. Linda, I thank you especially, for finding me. I love you all. Thank you."

Donna and I climbed on the plane the next day with a suitcase full of video tapes and film, some precious snapshots of my parents, my father's "strike alert" gadget, and enough memories to last a long, long time.

I also carried back a determination to track down some firm answers at last. Enough hints and guesses, I swore. I'd get my records from the welfare agency and find out the truth myself. But, as I was soon to find, if I thought my family was evasive, they were nothing compared to the bureaucracies of the New York state welfare system.

CHAPTER FOURTEEN

High Hopes and Stone Walls

Did my birth mother refuse to let me be adopted for so long because she kept hoping to take me back? If she did, why did she finally give up? Was she alive or dead? If she was dead, how did she die? If she was alive, where, and would she want to see me?

Back home, I waited a few weeks while things settled in my head, then I went looking for answers. There was no question about where to start. I'd seen it—the medallion with "Westchester Welfare Agency"—every time the grey car brought the Welfare Lady to our house or took one of us to the agency.

First I wrote the agency a letter—with my name, birth date, my foster family's name—asking for a copy of my file. When there was no reply after a month, I called. And called, and called. Each time I was shunted off to a new person, who was never available to talk on the phone but would call back if I left a message. Finally, on the fourth call, I got a real person on the phone. She had a pleasant voice, very cheery, but the minute I gave her my name she started coughing—"A-huh, a-huh"—a really phony cough.

"Excuse me," she said. "I've been out with bronchitis, I've been terribly sick. Can I call you back in a week or so?"

It was obvious that she recognized my name, knew why I was calling, and was stalling for time so she could figure out what to tell me. There wasn't much I could do about it, though, so I left my number one more time. Of course I never heard from her so I called her again.

This time the first thing I said was, "How are you feeling now?"

"Fine."

"That's good. Now. What's going on about my file? I've been writing and calling for two months and nobody will tell me anything."

"You've got to understand, Mr. Benzola, that was a long time ago, and you were a foster child, you were never adopted. We don't keep records like that, they're disposed of. There's a building where records are kept, but there are so many of them. Do you know what kind of a job it would be, looking through them?"

"No problem," I said. "I'll go through them myself, I'll fly back there and look through all of them if I have to. You can have somebody with me, watching, if you want."

"No, no. The chances are, I'll be honest with you, the files are destroyed. We just didn't keep files on foster children from that long ago. If you'd have been adopted it would have been different."

My blood really started to boil with that. "What's that supposed to mean? So my life wasn't worth anything because I wasn't adopted?"

"No, that's not it. But you have to understand, there were a lot of foster children at that time."

"You don't have to tell me. I *lived* with them. Mrs. Butler, my foster mother, took care of hundreds." She recognized the Butler name, and we began to talk about the agency doctors, seeing which ones we both knew about. The atmosphere relaxed a little.

"Look, Mr. Benzola. What I'm going to do . . . let me look around, see what I can find out, and I'll get back to you in a couple of days."

By then she was sounding like she might really do something. For the next few days I hung around the phone, waiting. I should have known better than to get my hopes up. After a week or so I called her again.

"Oh, um, yes. Mr. Benzola," she said, hemming and hawing. "Um, well, truthfully, there was a big fire over there at the records building. Your files were probably destroyed. That building burned down."

"Wait a minute! The other day, the last time we talked, you didn't know about any fire at that building."

"I just didn't think about it. All I have here on your case is a little index card. It has some information." She read off my birth parents' real names, my mother's address.

I told her I knew all that, what I needed was something that would help me find out about my mother. I decided to try taking a stab in the dark, based on some hints I'd gotten from the family in New York. "My mother had another child before me," I said, as if it was something I already knew for sure. "I want to find that person."

"Yes," the woman said, "his name is Benzola, too. But I can't give you the address, I'm not allowed to do that. I *can* tell you he's in Long Island."

My heart was pounding. It worked! And I did have another brother, one on my mother's side. I did my best to sound calmly curious. "Another one named Benzola . . . where did that name come from?"

"Your mother was married to a man named Benzola," the woman explained.

"You mean she was married to Benzola at the same time she had a boyfriend named Edward John Bednarczyk?"

"I don't know about that. But I imagine she was trying to protect you by giving you her husband's last name but the first two names of your natural father. That's probably what happened."

My heart was pounding. This new Benzola person could be holding all the answers about my—our—mother. But no matter what I said, the woman refused to give me his first name or his address. The most she would do is promise to write to him, and if he wanted to get in touch with me it would be his choice.

The second we got off the phone I called Linda in New York. "You said you wanted to help me find things out, right? So get every Long Island phone book. Find anybody with the name Benzola." Linda promised to get right on it, and it wasn't long before she called back. A George Benzola was listed.

There I was again, with the phone number of a person who might be part of my natural family, getting my nerve up to call across the continent.

But George Benzola wouldn't tell me anything I wanted to know. "I have no younger brother, none at all," he said flatly, when I reached him and introduced myself. "My mother and father are dead. There's nobody else." He refused to say anymore. "Good luck. I hope you find who you're looking for," he said, and hung up.

That seemed to be that. But was George Benzola lying, and he really is my brother? Why would he lie? Later, Linda tried visiting the agency in person to find out more. She actually got through to the Director, but he told her to mind her own business. They'd sent the man a letter, he didn't want to answer, and that was the end of it.

So the questions remain. The biggest, to me: is my natural mother alive, and if not, if she's dead, did she kill herself? My father did. I have a terrible suspicion that she did, too. That would explain why so many people I met in New York, who knew her, wouldn't tell me anything, just kept saying "You've been hurt enough already."

Linda, on her own, made one more try to get the truth for me. She went to a woman who'd been my mother's good friend. I'd talked to her when we were in New York, but she denied even knowing my mother. This time the woman admitted she remembered when I was born.

"Do you know if Lillian is still alive?" Linda asked bluntly.

"Lillian was always sickly," the woman said. "I think she's dead." And that's all Linda could get her to say.

—•—

It's hard. I want to know the truth. But I also have a terrible fear of what more I might find out. It seems like so many times, when I find answers, they're hard ones to hear.

My birth father's suicide, for instance. I'm sure now that I was part of the reason he killed himself, although I refused to admit it at first. I'm sure now that he knew I was alive all along, from something he said when my first wife Susan found him in 1978. He wasn't shocked to find out I was alive, he was upset that I was trying to find him. When she told him, the first thing he said wasn't, "My son is alive!" It was, "But I have a family now." And as his other children told me, from that time he just kept dragging down and down. That wasn't the only thing that made him take his life. But I can admit now that finding me was part of it.

Maybe if I find out more about my birth mother the same thing will happen. Like I said, I'm afraid of finding out that she killed herself, too. Then I'd have two birth parents who committed suicide. Sometimes I'm more afraid that she isn't dead, and I might find her only to have her slam the door in my face. Sometimes, I'm told, people find their parents but the parents don't want to know them. I've had the door slammed in my face too many times already.

Or maybe I'll find out she was a tramp. That one's been in my head since I was a child, along with all the sin talk from the Catholic school, and the other kids calling me "Bastard." Could I understand, forgive her, or would those old judgments come boiling back up?

But no matter how afraid I might be of the answers I might find, nobody has the right to keep them hidden from me. These are my own parents. I should be allowed to know as much about them as anybody knows about their parents. The welfare agency didn't protect me when I needed it, and they have no right to hide my own background in the name of protection now. I'm strong enough to find out more about my mother no matter what it might be.

I let it all go sometimes. But it always comes back. That's the killer. That's why more than anything I wanted my file. If I read it maybe I wouldn't need to go any further. I might find enough in there and I could say "That's it, that's enough," and I could quit.

I have already forgiven my father. I know that, when I get

the courage to find more answers about my natural mother, I can do the same for her. And for myself.

What I can't forgive or understand is the system that lets children live the way I did, and worse, then refuses to give them the information that would help them heal.

—•—

"Heal from what?" some people ask when I tell them my story. "Looks like you've done pretty well for yourself."

That makes me mad, but I can't blame them. Like I said at the beginning of this book, I thought the same way myself most of the time, until that day my sister Linda called. I knew I wasn't perfect, but I didn't really understand how much hurt I was carrying around inside or what it was doing to me. I was like somebody who'd been in a crash and looked okay on the outside but had awful internal injuries.

The most damaged part of me was—still is—the ability to be loving and affectionate. Susan, my ex-wife, was the first one to find that out. We got married right after Mom died, but our marriage was a struggle from the beginning. Inside, where most people feel love, I just had a hollow feeling. I didn't know how to love or show affection. I was afraid, for one thing, because getting close to people always wound up hurting. They always went away, like my foster brothers and sisters, or else they refused to have anything to do with me, like the Butlers' natural children. Susan tried hard, and so did her wonderful family, but our marriage was doomed from the start.

Susan knew what was wrong with me. That's why, just before we moved across the country to California, she investigated and found my birth father. She thought maybe if I found my own family I could relax and let myself feel better.

She had no way of knowing it would backfire, that time when she found my father and all he'd agree to was meeting me in a diner. Instead of finding a way to make me more open, it made me reject him and his puny little offer. It was one more brick in the wall I was building around myself and my feelings.

Susan and I divorced soon after that. Then I was *really* alone, the way I always dreaded. Booze was the first thing I tried to replace her with. Not "real" booze, I'd tell myself—just beer. But I managed to drink so much beer I was drunk most of the time for several months.

I know from reading that children of alcoholics often turn out to be alcoholics themselves. John Butler was one of the worst boozers I ever met. But maybe because he wasn't my natural father, or maybe just because he set such an ugly example, the drinking didn't stick, with me. I got disgusted with myself after a while and cut out the drinking-for-sorrow routine. Now I have an occasional beer, but it's never been a problem again.

After I gave up the booze things started to turn around for me. Business was going great. Ever since I was ten and started my bottle business, working and making money was my best way of making up for what was missing in my life. I'd always been able to talk, too, and get along with people. I turned out to be a good manager, and a good manager is always in demand.

Being successful in business was a real boost to me, but even better was meeting Donna and her two kids, Amy and Aaron, in 1983. She was going through a rough divorce, and she was from an alcoholic family too. But she was beautiful and smart, and a really nice woman. Her kids were great too, even though they were having a tough time with her divorce. We all had to learn to trust each other in order to get through that time, and we've been good together ever since.

Donna and I agreed not to have kids of our own. I was too scared. How could I give kids my name when I didn't even know where it came from? And what kind of inheritance would I be passing on? With as much trouble as I had in showing love, what kind of father could I be? It was hard enough learning how to be a father to Amy and Aaron.

In spite of our problems, Donna and I worked hard to make a go of things. She's just as stubborn as I am, and we turned out to be a good balance for each other. But I know that I'm not a great husband. It's hard for me to just give somebody a hug or a kiss or tell them how much I love them. When you're a foster kid, you might see the "real" kids in a family get the loving, but you don't get that for yourself. You don't know how it feels.

Knowing my natural family, being around them and seeing how they act with each other, has helped me start learning how to show my feelings with my wife and children. If the foster agency had their way, I never would have found them.

Growing up in foster care didn't leave me with broken bones from beatings, but it left me with a damaged body. The colitis I've had all my life will never be cured. There were just too many years of torment every night in the Hell Room. My stomach was in a knot a dozen times a day all my life, from fear and anger and needing things I couldn't get.

My bad knee might be the one thing my foster background doesn't have anything to do with. In fact, in a strange way it might be because of my knee that I'm finally finding things out about my family—and myself. I'd already had one knee operation when, in 1982, I was supervising the moving of one of my offices for my employer, when a truck operator misunderstood a signal and dropped a load of office equipment right on my knee.

It might sound odd, but horrible as that accident was (and still is) it also brought some good with the bad. Besides a financial settlement that left me comfortable for the rest of my life, it forced me to learn how to live without the usual distraction of business. When Linda's call came I was ready to follow it up.

Like I said, it makes me mad when people say growing up in foster care can't be so bad. Millions of other foster kids aren't as lucky as I was. All anybody has to do is look on the street or in a homeless shelter to see a lot of the unluckier ones. According to studies, almost half of the homeless people were once in foster care. You can find a lot of ex-foster children in prisons, too.

I never forget that some of them are the babies I once helped take care of.

CHAPTER FIFTEEN

A Deadly Silence

So far I've been writing about foster care from the inside, as I lived it. I've also read a lot of books and reports about it—most of them by "experts" looking at foster care from the outside; social workers, psychologists, members of government investigating panels. No matter where we're looking at it from, the experts and I agree about one thing, at least.

The American foster care system is a mess.
It was already a mess in 1980 when a Federal Adoption Assistance and Child Welfare Act was passed, requiring specific reforms in foster care. Eight years later, when Congress investigated again, they found:

> ". . . agencies in crisis and services that are failing families and children. The promise

extended almost ten years ago has not been kept, and children are paying the price . . . We found extraordinary failings in these systems that remain within our capacity to control. Federal oversight and funding are weak to nonexistent." (*No Place to Call Home: Discarded Children in America*, A Report of the Select Committee on Children, Youth, and Families, U.S. House of Representatives.)

No matter how many studies are done and reports are written, the system just keeps grinding away. In the beginning of this book I mentioned the "Little Hoover Commission" that investigated the foster care system in California. Two years after the federal reform act was passed, that state had passed its own set of laws to improve foster care. When the Commission reviewed the state of foster care it found that:

"There have been few indications that the foster care system has improved; indeed, all signs point to a worsening of conditions."

What does "worsening conditions" mean? For a huge number of foster children it means pain, terror, and even death. California child welfare officials estimate that about 10% of the state's foster children are abused—but, as the Commission points out, since this only counts the problems *reported* ". . . such an estimate is a highly suspect figure given the lack of a good, unbiased reporting mechanism."

In other words, The Commission was convinced that *more than* 10% of foster children are abused.

And how many is that, nationwide? Again, nobody knows for sure because nobody keeps track, but with the best guess at 300,000-500,000 American children in foster care, it's probably safe to say that at any given time 30,000 are being abused—beaten, starved, tortured, raped, even murdered—not by maniacs on a killing spree, but by people hired to "protect" them by our own government.

If everybody knows how bad things are, and everybody agrees about at least some of the ways they can be changed, why does foster care keep getting worse?

Part of the reason, I think, is that these terrible things happen in private, inside the walls of foster homes. Most of the time nobody even notices. The children know that, just like I did. It's almost the worst part of being a foster child— knowing that nobody cares. Nobody is going to save you.

Suppose all those children could be brought to the same baseball stadium. Put the ones who are being starved in one section, the ones being raped in another, the ones being used in child-pornography in another. Down on the field put the ones being beaten and let the TV cameras broadcast as they're hit and kicked and whipped—maybe have some portable closets for the ones who are locked up in the dark. If you could do that, things would change. But as long as children are suffering in silence, hidden away, it's too easy for them to be ignored.

Once in a while one of the horror stories does come out. A few days before writing this chapter, for instance, I read in Anna Quindlen's *New York Times* column about a five year old girl who sounded a lot like Peter, my foster brother I told about earlier who set himself on fire. Like Peter, this little girl had been sent from one foster home to another—

she, too, was "difficult to love." She'd do things like stealing and defecating on the floor, maybe to get attention. The girl died, beaten to death by her foster mother's twenty-year-old son, "Another child dead under the not-so-watchful eye of the city of New York," as Quindlen put it. The man who killed her was sentenced to one and a third to four years.

More tens of thousands of foster children escape physical abuse but are tortured in other ways every day. What happens to them might not be as violent, but it will do almost as much damage. These are the ones who watch their foster families' "real" children be given love, toys, birthday parties, cuddling and hugs and wonder what's wrong with them that they don't get such things. The pain of it won't kill them outright, but it can cripple them just as surely as if they were physically tortured.

It's no wonder that so many foster children grow up and live lonely or violent lives. As one former foster care caseworker is quoted in Quindlen's column, "Sometimes I see one of those really horrible crimes on TV and everyone is saying 'how could a human being do that? And my mind thinks 'maybe it was one of my children.' With how they lived, they could wind up doing anything."

Everybody knows how much it can hurt a child to lose a parent in a divorce. Almost nobody stops to think how much more foster children hurt, even though they've lost at least their two natural parents and sometimes up to a dozen foster parents. When children go through that much pain they can't grow up and lead normal lives. But even when they end up in a news report about some horrible crime, the fact that they were once foster children is usually ignored—it might be mentioned in passing, but nobody ever seems to draw any conclusions from it.

A few months ago I clipped another story from the *New York Times* about an older man who had been "rescued" from his homeless life on the New York streets and taken to a work-training farm in the country. The article told his life story, including how he'd grown up in foster care, and raved about how well he did in the program, how intelligent and quick to learn he was. Everything was going so well with him that the program considered him its biggest success—until he walked away from it one day and went back to his former way of life. "He just seemed to be a loner," the program people said with regret. "We're not sure why." He didn't seem to like living in the dormitory, was uncomfortable being part of a group, they said. The article didn't make any connection between this man's choice and his foster care childhood. But it's no mystery to me that somebody who grew up an outcast would only be comfortable as an outcast for the rest of his life.

Thank heaven I had Mrs. Butler as a foster mother, who could keep me with her and give me the strength to survive. But even so, as I said earlier and as anybody close to me can tell you, I've got plenty of my own kind of scars from it. Besides the ones I've talked about already, something is always happening to remind me of how different my life has been. Sometimes I see people looking through their family albums, smiling at the good memories it brings back. When I look through albums from growing up at the Butler's, I see pictures of people who never belonged to me, babies and kids I lost and never saw again, birthday parties that were never for me. It still hurts, and it always will.

The longer a child spends in foster care the more damage the system does to them. Foster children are already hurting emotionally or physically or both because they've lost their birth families, but the system doesn't offer them much help.

"Longterm foster care can leave lasting psychological scars . . . .More than 50% of the children in foster care are in this 'temporary' status for over six years, over 30% are away from their parents for over six years . . . While in foster care, children are supposed to receive treatment services to remedy the effects of past maltreatment. Few do." (Encyclopedia Britannica Research Papers)

Dozens of people reported the same kind of things to Congress in the 1988 hearings. All but two of them were child welfare professionals from social services agencies, children's advocate groups, government bureaus and so on. The other two were like me; they'd learned about foster care the hard way, by being in it themselves. They talked about their loneliness and how hard it was to be sent from family to family, the mental abuse and physical abuse they suffered. The professionals talked about things like "appropriate mental health services," "poor family functioning," and "basic services responsibilities." Underneath it all the message was the same; too many kids hurting, too little being done about it.

Stuck in a miserable failure of a system with no hope of help, many children take *themselves* out of foster care as soon as they get old enough. In California, 45% of runaways have been in foster care (Little Hoover Commission); in New York as many as 50% of homeless youths have been in foster care (Congressional Report). Children lead miserable lives on the streets—but to many, even the street seems better than their foster homes.

—•—

The worst part of all this, to me, is that foster care doesn't have to be that bad. Maybe it can't ever be perfect, but you don't have to have a degree in social work to know how to make it a lot better:

1. Fewer children
2. In better care
3. For shorter times.

We need to have fewer children born to parents who can't take care of them. There's no big secret about how to do it. We need more sex education to keep people from having unprotected, casual sex; plenty of cheap or free contraceptives; and for those who get pregnant anyway and choose it, abortion. When we have all those things the number of children without families will be a fraction as many.

People who object to the abortion part of this sometimes come at me with what they think is the clincher, "You say you're for abortion, but what if your mother had aborted *you*?" My answer, from the bottom of my heart, is, "She should have. So should the mothers of Peter and Judy and lots of the other foster children I knew, instead of putting us through lives like that." These people make the mistake of thinking there would be a "me" to regret being aborted, but that's nonsense. Of course I don't want anybody to take my life now, but that's another question.

We can cut down on the number of foster children by giving services to help keep families together. Simple lack

113

of money for basic necessities—particularly health care—forces poor parents to give up their children just because they're sick, or have some other temporary emergency. When you have barely enough money to scrape by, any problem at all can tear your family apart. If a poor parent loses an apartment or a job or health, they often lose their families too. And once your children are in the foster care system, it's very hard to get them back.

Some parents put children in foster care because that's the only way the children can get some kinds of therapy. Some go into foster care because their parents are the ones who need treatment for drugs or alcohol and can't get it. If we cared about families we'd give people help without forcing them to give up their children first.

It's true that no matter how we might cut down on the number of children in foster care, there will always be some who need temporary families. Maybe the parents have a serious illness, or die in an accident, and there aren't any relatives to take the children. For the ones who really do need foster care, it should be as good as it can possibly be. They already have enough pain from losing their parents.

The federal government needs to set up a central agency to keep track of the system and enforce basic standards. A lot of people scream about state's rights and not wanting more bureaucracy when they hear this. But even horse races are better regulated than foster care. As Anna Quindlen said about the little girl who was beaten to death, "If the Sanitation Department had this poor a record on trash collection, we would be up in arms." We insist on federal testing for drugs, meat quality, and bug spray—so I think we can insist on at least a little federal control of the people who are supposed to take care of foster children.

States must make the system simpler and set up coordination among foster care agencies. The system itself abuses children. In many California counties the process for bringing a new foster child into the system takes *". . . as many as 22 child welfare professionals, each of whom must interview and review a child's case separately."* (Little Hoover Commission)

The cost of such a system in dollars is bad enough, but imagine what the children go through! That's nothing but bureaucratic torture, and there's no excuse for it.

It's even wrong to talk about such a mess as a "system," because there's really no system to it at all. Once in a while, bad foster parents are caught and lose their license to take children, but all they have to do is move and apply to take children in another county or state. There should be a central agency that keeps records on every past and present foster parent, with fingerprints.

Foster parents should be carefully screened, trained, and supported with counseling. Being a foster parent is one of the hardest jobs there is—just like anybody else applying for an important job, they have to be checked out very carefully.

This week there's a front page story in my local newspaper about a foster mother who is suspected of killing three babies and intentionally injuring at least eight others of the forty foster children she's had in the last eight years. Officials suspect the woman has something called "Munchausen's Syndrome by Proxy," a psychological disorder that drives people to injure children in order to gain a doctor's sympathy and attention. Was this woman screened before she was licensed to take care of foster children? Did anybody give her psychological tests to see if she was emotionally fit? Probably not. In this state there are no laws or rules that call for psychological testing of people who want to be foster parents.

(This is another example, too, of what happens because the foster system is so confused and uncoordinated. You might think that someone would have noticed something was wrong when so many children were sick or dying in this foster home. Nobody did because the woman was getting children from many different agencies. None of them had the whole picture. Babies would still be dying in that home, if a doctor hadn't noticed that the woman was bringing too many babies to the hospital.)

Once would-be foster parents are screened to weed out the worst risks, they have to be trained. At least teach them how not to hurt their foster children thoughtlessly. The foster fathers need to be trained as well as the mothers—I know foster families where the mothers work hard to make it good, just like mine did, but the father either stays out of it or makes it hard for her. The father is often the one who brings up the difference between foster children and "real" children. "Now you get off the bike, that's Johnny's." They might not be mean, they might just not understand how that feels to a child who's already hurting from losing a family. Foster parents can't take care of really hard-case children without plenty of counseling and help.

Most foster parents don't get any training at all, or get only a few hours. In California, almost 35% get none, about 20% get about twelve hours, and only 10% get more training than that. (Little Hoover Commission) A recommended amount is at least thirty hours of training for new foster parents and at least that much again every year.

There are many good foster parents; warm, caring people who make great sacrifices for the children in their care. From everything I've read, most of these great people do a good job in spite of the system, not because of it.

116

We need more caseworkers, and more supervision of foster homes. One person can't even keep track of as many foster children as most caseworkers handle, let alone inspect the homes to be sure they're doing a good job. New York has the second highest number of foster children in the nation; according to Congressional testimony, its Special Services for Children is ". . . severely overburdened, understaffed, and in crisis. Workers remove children from their homes because there is not enough time to do a proper investigation and because they lack time to follow-up since their caseloads are so high . . . staff turnover at CPS was almost 70% in 1987."

When social workers are under that kind of pressure, how on earth can they do a good job? They don't have time to visit all their cases, to make sure things are all right, or help out when there's a problem. If a caseworker had been able to do regular inspections of foster homes, would the little girl that Anna Quindlen wrote about have been saved?

True, it's hard to balance between having enough inspection of foster homes to protect children, and having so much inspection that the family's rights are abused. In my county a group of foster parents has joined to protest against what they call "Gestapo tactics" by agency inspectors. They accuse the agency of barging into their homes without notice, putting everybody through the third degree, and treating foster parents like criminals. This is a real problem, but I don't see any choice, unless the system is improved. The inspection "raids" in my county were started because foster abuse was getting so bad it couldn't be ignored. A policeman told me in private that one of the foster mothers was well known to be "turning out" her teenage foster daughters as prostitutes. The agency kept on sending her new ones, whenever the others ran away or got too old, he said. He pointed her out as one of the parents protesting loudest about the inspections.

Too much inspection can be hard, but I think it's better than too little. The problems in foster homes have gone on so long that probably the good foster parents will have to suffer through more inspections until the system gets better.

Foster care agencies shouldn't be allowed to operate in secret, pretending they're protecting the children or families' privacy. As it is, the agencies can get away with just about anything. Nobody ever knows, because the records are sealed. The only ones the agencies are really protecting are themselves. The rights of the children come last, if they come at all. How could it protect foster children to hide what happened to the little girl in New York? It might be necessary to hide the identities of the people, but not what they did—or didn't do, especially the agency itself.

I'm convinced that the Westchester Welfare Agency lied to me about my own records being burned. I believe they're afraid I'll find something wrong in those files and make trouble for them. But even if that's not true, if they're really trying to protect my mother's privacy and not their own, whose rights are more important, hers or mine? In this case, I believe mine are. The natural parents of foster children shouldn't be allowed to get out of at least that one duty to the babies they put into the world. Whatever their reasons for giving up their children, once those children are grown up they should be able to go back and find out who they came from. We should be able to read about our birth parents and find out about our genetic inheritance to protect our future children or our own health. We should be able to find out about our pasts to help us lose the awful feeling of being nobodies, belonging to no one. We might not like what we find out but we can get over that, with help. How can we get over something we never know?

I said earlier that I'm afraid of some of the answers I might find when I finally do get to see my foster care records. But I know that I will keep trying. I hope every other adult foster child who reads this will be pushing to get their own answers. The system has done enough to us already; the least it can give us is the truth about our own lives.

As I said in the beginning of this book, I hid my background and my pain from everybody, even myself, for many years. Bringing it out has helped me. I hope other adult foster children will come forward too. Maybe if enough of us are willing to face our pain and make it public, we can start changing things for the other temporary children. If we don't, who will?

EPILOGUE

from Neva Beach

For Ed Benzola, writing this book was like deliberately walking—again and again—into the darkest, most monster-ridden closet a child ever imagined in the night. Except for him the monsters were real. Most of us develop a set of familiar memories, an edited version of our life we can refer to without too much discomfort. Ed set out to go behind the easy memories and look at the ones that were still alive, still fresh and potent with pain. My respect for his courage and integrity grew as he faced each new chapter. He often flinched, but he never lied and he refused to hide.

Before meeting Ed and working with him on this book, I thought about foster care the way most people probably do—which is not much at all. If I saw a TV news story about a fire or drug raid or car crash that ended with "The children are in foster care," that was that, for me. The loose ends had been tied up. The children, I assumed, although no doubt lonely and scared, were safely installed with some generous couple who would see them through the pain and help them build good new lives.

Now I know better. Ed's story and our research have made it impossible to hear "The children are in foster care" as anything but a sentence. I know that a lucky few will go through the foster system with only a few, perhaps unavoidable, scars. But most will do "hard time" as surely as any prison-bound felon. For some, foster care will be a death sentence.

He often talks about not understanding what love is, but I have come to believe that Ed Benzola is one of the most loving people I know. He may not be much good at hugs and stroking, but—as this book shows—there's nothing wrong with his ability to cherish and care for other people. He has taught me that I can't take foster care for granted, that everyone who cares about children has to start fighting for them. I have, and I hope you will too.

from Ed Benzola

Writing this book over the past year and a half has been one of the most challenging and emotional experiences of my life. Many old wounds were re-opened as I faced memories and emotions I had never let myself fully feel before. And as I researched five decades of foster care and read about the millions of other foster children, I couldn't help sharing their loneliness and pain too.

I still find myself trying to understand this thing called "love." The big wall inside me keeps trying to rebuild itself but some of it is down for good, and the cracks in the rest of it have started to get wider and deeper. My goal is to finally see the whole wall come down and stay that way. Only then will I understand what love is, and be able to feel and give it fully.

I hope you have been able to live, even for a short time, in "little Eddie's" skin. I know that until people understand what it is like to be a foster child, nothing will be changed. If you have been touched by anything in my story, I hope you will be moved to join the fight to change the foster care system.

As I finish the book, I still have no idea if my natural mother, Lillian Barry, is living or dead. If she is alive I say to her, "If you are out there I hope you will let me know in some way. There is so much I want to know, about my father, about my other sibling, about you. I would like to meet you, and then I can finally close this chapter of my life."

To the other foster children who were part of my life at the Butlers'—Peter, Francine, Gerard, Charlie, and the rest of you, "Oh, how I miss you, and how often I've wanted to know how you are and what has become of you. If any part of this story sounds familiar to you, please get in touch. I would love to hear from you."

And lastly, to everyone else who is or has been a "temporary child," I think about you all the time. Each of you is a unique and valuable person, and don't ever let anybody tell you different. Life may not have dealt us a fair hand, but we have the power to make up for that and change this system.

Bibliography

Works Cited

Encyclopedia Britannica, 1990: Vol. 19, "Family and Kinship;" Vol. 27, "Family Welfare."

Encyclopedia Britannica Research Papers, 1992: "Running Away From Home," "Explanation of Adoption," "Adopting a Child," "Foster Care Programs for Children."

Felker, Evelyn. *Foster Parenting Young Children.* New York, Child Welfare League of America, 1974. Niles, Reg. *The Reg Niles Search Book for Adult Adoptees.* Phileas Deight, 1978.

Bibliography

U.S. House of Representatives, Select Committee on Children, Youth, and Families. *No Place To Call Home: Discarded Children in America:* Hearings of April 13, 1988, April 28, 1988, May 12, 1988, November, 1989.

Other Sources

Academic American Encyclopedia. 1991, Prodigy Interactive Personal Service, "Adoption and Foster Care." 1991

Birch, Jennings. *They Cage the Animals at Night.* New York, New American Library, 1984.

Jones, E.P. *Where is Mom?* New York. Four Walls, Eight Windows. 1990.

Ryan, Jillian and Joseph. *Please, Somebody, Love Me!* Grand Rapids, Baker Book House, 1991.

State of California, Little Hoover Commission. *Mending Our Broken Children.* 1992.

Taylor, Ronald B. *The Kid Business.* Boston, Houghton Mifflin Co., 1981.

I would like to hear from other people about their experiences with foster care. Please write to me c/o:
Real People Publishing

Edward J. Benzola
5778 Bellflower Drive
Newark, Ca 94560
ebenzola@sbcglobal.net
510-791-2452